LOST AND FOUND

Real Stories of Broken Lives Restored in Northeast Indiana

Published in Beaverton, Oregon, by Good Catch Publishing.
www.goodcatchpublishing.com
V1.1

Printed in the United States of America

Table of Contents

DEDICATION

This book is dedicated to all those who have lost something of extreme value in life. Perhaps you've lost a loved one, a job, your reputation, your identity or even all your hope. If you feel like your life needs to be restored in a significant way, then this book is for you!

ACKNOWLEDGEMENTS

I would like to thank Stuart Kruse for his vision for this book and for his hard work in making it a reality. And to the people of County Line, thank you for your boldness and vulnerability in sharing your personal stories.

This book would not have been published without the amazing efforts of our project manager and editor, Hayley Pandolph. Her untiring resolve pushed this project forward and turned it into a stunning victory. Thank you for your great fortitude and diligence. Deep thanks to our incredible Editor in Chief, Michelle Cuthrell, and Executive Editor, Jen Genovesi, for all the amazing work they do. I would also like to thank our invaluable proofreader, Melody Davis, for the focus and energy she has put into perfecting our words.

Lastly, I want to extend our gratitude to the creative and very talented Jenny Randle, who designed the beautiful cover for *Lost and Found: Real Stories of Broken Lives Restored in Northeast Indiana.*

Daren Lindley
President and CEO
Good Catch Publishing

The book you are about to read
is a compilation of authentic life stories.
The facts are true, and the events are real.
These storytellers have dealt with crisis, tragedy, abuse
and neglect and have shared their most private moments,
mess-ups and hang-ups in order for others to learn and
grow from them. In order to protect the identities of those
involved in their pasts, the names and details of some
storytellers have been withheld or changed.

INTRODUCTION

No matter where you live, you're bound to have experienced some type of loss. Our communities of Auburn, Garrett, Butler, Leo, Huntertown, Fort Wayne, etc., are no different, are we? The stories you are about to read are from people who live right here in our surrounding communities — they might even live next door to you!

Much like the open doors on the cover of this book, life is full of potential doors. The doors you choose can drastically alter the direction of your life. Discover how these people found hope in the midst of hopelessness. How they found restoration when life was destroyed. These are stories of real people who were once captive to despair, but are now living with hope and a purpose. If you could use some encouragement that life can and will gct better, you picked up the right book!

GLAD RECRUIT
The Story of JT King
Written by Douglas Abbott

"This could be it," I said aloud as I sat on my bed, exhausted but unable to sleep. On my lap was a 9mm handgun. I could feel the comforting weight of it on my thighs. The silver finish glinted in the light of my bedside lamp. I picked the gun up, fondled it and spun the cylinder, hearing the clicking of metal on metal. I flipped the cylinder out, deriving a dark pleasure from the fresh rounds I saw in the chambers. I spun it again and flipped it back into place. It was solid and handsome, a marvelous feat of manufacturing. I had fired it at the range several times and always kept it clean and oiled. There was approximately zero chance that it would fail to send a slug of lead into my brain.

I hadn't known it was possible for a human being to feel such a weight of sorrow, so much worse for the fact that it was of my own making. I was utterly alone. I had failed my family and every real friend I had. No one was left but a collection of chattering fools, every one eager to make use of my seemingly unlimited party funds. The drugs and the drink scarcely dulled the pain of a life which, from all appearances, was a cosmic accident. It was all a mad swirl of girls and money and fast cars — none of it amounting to a moment of real satisfaction. I was only

20, and life stretched before me like an unimaginably long prison sentence.

I lifted the gun to my temple experimentally. *No. Might not be enough to do the trick.* I lowered it a few inches, turned the barrel and considered placing it in my mouth. I could almost feel the metal clicking on my teeth — could almost taste the coppery gun oil on my tongue. With my forefinger, I pulled the hammer down, hearing the firing pin snap into place. All set. I put my thumb on the trigger …

శ్రీ శ్రీ శ్రీ

I had an idyllic childhood, though I wouldn't have said so at the time. It was a simple life of baseball practice, homeschool lessons and frolicking in the country where my family lived. My earliest memories are of sharing a duplex in Saint Joe, Indiana, with my grandparents, them on one side and my family on the other. My grandfather's cancer (and later a stroke suffered by my grandmother) had stolen their self-sufficiency, so my parents bought the duplex to keep them close.

My mom was strong as steel. She was a housewife, mother of four, homeschool teacher and part-time care provider for my grandparents. I still don't know how she did it all. Adversity and the demands of life made her something of a pistol, but there was no question that she loved all of us. Her love language was *doing*. We lacked for nothing that was in her power to provide for us.

My father was the sole breadwinner and was gone most of the time. Hence, it fell to my much-older sisters (eight and nine years my senior) to help keep things buttoned up.

There was little time for discussion when one of us misbehaved. Real-time discipline usually amounted to my being summarily confined to my room. The law of our home was gentleness in speech and in actions toward others. It was a moral code that required little enforcement, mainly because my parents were the first to practice it.

I went to a public middle school and soon noticed with displeasure all the amenities my schoolmates enjoyed that were forbidden to me. For my siblings and me, our entertainment choices, films, music artists and leisure activities were all scrutinized and sharply limited.

One day, I came in the door, set down an armload of books and popped into the kitchen, where my mom was cutting vegetables at the sink.

"Hi, Mom. Kyle invited me to his birthday party. He's having a sleepover."

"Kyle who?"

"Kyle Armstrong."

"We don't know the Armstrongs."

"What's to know? They're not devil worshippers or anything. They're nice people."

My mom shot me a look. "I don't care how nice they are. We don't know them, so the answer is *no*."

"You're making it so I have no social life."

LOST AND FOUND

"You're about to have even less of a social life — like from the inside of your room. How does that work for you?"

ॐॐॐ

Middle school brought me the social life I'd been wanting. My sports prowess and a good dose of charm made me popular in school. Between my athletic ability and the small size of our country school, I stood out easily on my baseball and basketball teams. My father always cheered me on and inquired regularly about our exploits. He even attended some of the important games whenever he could.

During my sophomore year in high school, a friend named Brent turned me onto Limewire. Soon I was downloading all my favorite music. One day I was doing this on my parents' computer at home when a video popped up. I watched, entranced, as a gorgeous young woman gyrated on the computer screen without a stitch of clothing on. I had never seen anything like it. I knew instantly that watching it was wrong. The images carried dark, heavy vibrations. However, I also felt my body responding. It felt powerful and good, and I immediately went back for more. Brent had showed me how to erase the Internet history on the browser.

I knew I couldn't talk to my parents about this. Downloading pirated music was bad enough, but I had now repeatedly downloaded porn videos. However, the decision was taken out of my hands not long afterward when, following a downloading session, I forgot to log off Limewire. One of my parents' employees discovered the browser trail and brought it to their attention. My parents were caught completely off guard.

"I can't believe you would use our equipment to watch that putrid crap!" My mom was livid.

"It happened by accident," I protested, describing how the first video had popped up on the screen.

"It happened by accident seven times?" my dad said. "That's how many sites we found in the browser history. And that was just that session."

I could think of nothing to say.

"Of course it feels good to watch that stuff," my dad said, his hands in his pockets. "You're a healthy young man. But sex isn't supposed to be the way you see it presented in these smut features. Sex is about loving a woman and holding her with gentleness. These porn videos present women like they were consumer products. It's really bad stuff."

"I didn't mean for this to happen," I said lamely.

"Well, you can think about it while you're on computer restriction for the next six months!" my mom snapped.

I felt the truthfulness of their convictions, but I was overpowered by the animal pleasure I had discovered. It was only the latest casualty of my burgeoning independence, thanks to which I was finding all kinds of glittering toys in the world beyond my parents' purview. I sensed that my parents' strict rules were well-intentioned, but I had long felt that they were excessively stifling. It didn't need to be pointed out to me that their authority over me was waning quickly simply because of my age.

I landed a job doing custom truck detailing later that year. I was a shoe-in because of my skills with tools. The job created a kind of shotgun emancipation in my life because of the big income I was earning, which led quickly to my obtaining my license and my first vehicle. The protective cocoon my parents had so carefully constructed around me began to disintegrate quickly.

When the job turned full time, I stopped attending school and continued my studies at home to accommodate my work schedule. I was finding my own space in the world. The moral capital I had inherited from my parents kept me mostly out of trouble, but little by little, my boundaries began to morph. I began to fill my roster with a variety of characters and to conceal co-ed socials from my parents whenever they asked me questions about my activities.

A few months after I graduated, my parents went on a trip, leaving me in charge of the house. The evening after seeing them off at the airport, I was standing in my living room with 20 of my friends. Each of us was clutching a bottle of beer, while rock music shook the rafters.

About halfway through the evening, Charles approached me. He had just arrived at the party.

"Hey, Charles! Glad you could make it."

"Hey, JT," he said with a wan look on his face.

"Have a beer." I gestured with my own bottle toward the refrigerator.

"No, thanks. Hey, I wanted to talk to you. My sister, Amanda, was pretty upset when she heard about this party. A friend of hers told her about the beer and stuff. Man, are your parents aware of what's going on here?"

I winced. Blasted small-town gossip mill. "Yeah, they know," I lied. "Listen, don't worry about it, man. We're all adults."

"Well, not everyone. There are some minors here. Anyway, I think Amanda is going to have some words for you."

Amanda did, in fact, have some words for me. She and a dozen other kids in their late teens formed the nucleus of a social circle I had been involved with for years. They didn't drink or use drugs. There wasn't a whiff of impropriety among them with regard to sex. They were ridiculed as "holy rollers" by the drinking set, but I immensely enjoyed the time I had spent with them. I found them to be honest, dependable people who had managed to sidestep the whole high school rat race.

Amanda approached me the next day at my workplace.

"JT, most of my friends are disappointed that you would throw a beer party at your parents' house. I am, too."

"Maybe it was a mistake," I said, feeling a little guilty.

"It definitely was a mistake. I can't believe you would do that while your parents are out of the country. Besides, what about your younger brother? Did you think about him at all?"

The exchange was my first informal notification that I had been excommunicated from the wholesome set that had been my primary peer group for most of my adolescence.

By this time, most of the people in my life were teenagers who drank, used drugs and approached sex as though it were another form of entertainment. Walking on the wild side was still new enough to be enjoyable, and my dabbling never affected my work performance.

I started to hear alarm bells, however, the weekend I lost my virginity. It happened with Melissa, a girl I had been going out with for several months. Afterward, I felt remorse like a steel blade in my gut. Ever since I had reckoned with the concept of sex and marriage as a pubescent teenager, I had carried a firm resolve to save myself for marriage. It was not only my parents' conviction, it was my own.

The worst part was that my decision to have sex had trashed Melissa's virtue as well. She had consented to sex because she loved me and wanted to please me. She had even looked up to me. I couldn't escape the harsh implications in my own analysis of the matter: I was a user who had taken the virginity of a trusting teenage girl.

Melissa was sweet and good-natured. In her heart, what happened between us meant we would most likely end up being husband and wife. I had feelings for Melissa, but I had no intention of marrying her. I actually believed that my hesitation about marriage was somehow more valid than the feelings of a billion randy, irresponsible teenagers who had come along before me. I began to pull away from her, not because I didn't respect her, but because I *did*. I couldn't bear to look into her soft, vulnerable eyes. The shattered purity I saw in them shot daggers into my soul.

Melissa felt abandoned as my emotional distance from her increased. I couldn't express to her that my unwillingness to be with her was based on my own failure. We never discussed the destructive meaning of our decision to sleep together until much later. Instead, we fought over everyday trifles. I wanted to forget the whole unpleasant spectacle.

I picked up the phone and dialed her number.

"Hello?"

"Melissa, I've been doing a lot of thinking. I'm not sure we should be together anymore."

"Oh, you're breaking up with me now?"

"It's not like I want to; we're just not getting along."

"Whose fault is that? You've been acting like a real p****."

"Well, you haven't been the most pleasant person in the world, either."

"I can't believe this. I thought you were a man. You're just like all the other jerks out there. I'm sorry I ever met you." And she hung up.

My personal boundaries were falling like dominoes. Soon, my drinking accelerated and marijuana was added to my daily repertoire. At the same time, my college plans were supplanted after a single semester by a generous promotion at my job. Among my fair-weather friends, I was considered a mover and a shaker who had everything that mattered in life: a license, a beautiful car, a cushy job and plenty of money to spend on beer and weed. I didn't realize it at the time, but my whole social life had turned into a series of testosterone contests. Every social gathering was a competition to see which man-boy could flash the most money, use the most drugs, drink more profusely and get the trophy girl. I took up the cause with gusto and intentionally filled my life with young people who did the same. I purposely pursued girls with relaxed sexual boundaries who weren't looking for emotional attachment. Everything in my life and daily schedule was there to satisfy my dull personal desires.

All the while, I felt a sadness welling up inside me. The skills and the drive I possessed had made me wildly successful, but I wasn't enjoying it much. I had embraced the freedom of adulthood, but the voices of my parents haunted me. I had managed to abandon everything they had taught me to value.

I resolved to make a clean break and seek counsel. For some reason, I didn't approach the leadership of my own church. Instead, I called Pastor Michaels, who was the leader of a church in Fort Wayne, whose youth group made up the majority of the social enclave from which I had been ostracized over the drinking party. I remembered the untroubled days and nights I had once enjoyed with them. I longed to be a part of the group again, recalling how its members had seemed to enjoy all life had to offer.

When I had asked to be allowed back before, Pastor Michaels had told me, "Frankly, there's an issue of trust now. I have an obligation to guard my flock, and I take it seriously. I'll need to see evidence of your sincere intentions before I allow you back."

He had gone on to set a whole list of requirements before me, including an oral confession before the entire group. At the time, meeting such a requirement had seemed out of the question. Now, however, I had a strong desire to be a part of the group again. I thought being around them might be instrumental in helping me to escape the vortex of substance abuse and promiscuity.

Pastor Michaels and I met at his home office around noon. He sat down behind his desk without offering me a refreshment.

"What brings you in today, JT?"

"Pastor, you know all about the party I threw at my parents' house and that there was drinking involved." He nodded.

"Well, things have gotten much worse since then. I've been drinking regularly and experimenting with drugs."

"What kinds of drugs?" he interjected.

"Pot. Cocaine. Narcotic pain pills." He crossed his arms and waited for me to continue.

"I've lost my virginity."

"How did this happen?"

I related the events surrounding my decision to sleep with Melissa.

"I know you just turned 18. How old is this girl?"

"She's 16. Nearly 17."

He exhaled audibly but didn't speak for several moments.

"JT, you've just told me you slept with an underage girl. I may have no choice but to report you to the authorities."

I was speechless.

Pastor Michaels placed his fingertips together and looked at me solemnly. "I've known you for a long time. I've known your parents even longer. I know they are both committed Christians. I'm disappointed that you would choose such a path for your life. I know your parents must be hurt by your rebellion."

He reached onto a shelf behind his desk and pulled down a thick Bible. He set it on his desk and began flipping through it. It seemed as though I could hear accusation in the rustling of the pages.

"JT, God's part is to reveal the truth to us. Our part is to run with it. I have no doubt that you know perfectly well what you're supposed to be doing. Your behavior is troubling."

He looked down at his Bible and began to recite a passage from the book of Hebrews:

"It is impossible for those who have once been enlightened, who have tasted the heavenly gift, who have shared in the Holy Spirit, who have tasted the goodness of the word of God and the powers of the coming age, if they fall away, to be brought back to repentance. To their loss they are crucifying the Son of God all over again and subjecting him to public disgrace."

He leaned back in his chair and let the passage sink in for a moment.

"I sincerely hope that's not you," he said sternly, poking the page in front of him. "If I were you, I'd be just about living on my knees. You need to pray and beg God to give you another chance. The scriptures say, 'Seek the Lord while he may be found.' If you mess up again, JT, it might be your last run."

I was undone as I walked out of his house. The pastor's words had struck me down. It was as though everything in existence had turned against me. The crisp blue sky, the warmth of the sun, the sharp notes of birdsong coming from the trees — all seemed to mock me. None of it was for me anymore. Worst of all, I felt I couldn't make use of the dire warnings he had given me. I knew the story of Jesus coming to earth to die for me, to cover all the wrong I'd done. Was it possible I had maxed out the number of bad things I was allowed to do in my life? I was convinced I had burned my bridges irrevocably.

ৡৡৡ

I was contemplating suicide. The impulse wasn't precisely proactive. It was simply all that remained after everything I thought worthwhile had been obliterated in my life. My moral and spiritual convictions had come to ruin. For many months, I had plodded through life without tasting anything enjoyable. Everything I had worked so hard for had turned stale. I wore my body out working each day under a boss I couldn't please for money that wasn't rewarding. I had no meaningful connection with my party friends and felt unworthy to be involved socially with the people who used to be part of my life. My parents listened compassionately, but I hadn't leveled with them about what I was going through. I expected nothing but harsh words from them. My reticence kept my entire family at an emotional distance. I was trapped in a social netherworld of my own making. I could feel the loneliness in my bones.

At night, as soon as I stopped moving, anxiety would strike, often preventing me from sleeping. I consumed copious amounts of alcohol and smoked a lot of weed simply to increase my chances of finding sleep. I was tormented.

When I was driving on the highway, I had frequent thoughts of swerving into oncoming traffic. I often imagined myself swallowing handfuls of pills, which I could easily obtain. Then I would simply go to sleep and never wake up. These dark ideas were my constant companions. During nights when sleep eluded me, I thought about the loaded 9mm handgun in the drawer of my nightstand. Finally one night, around 2 a.m., I pulled it out, cradled it in my lap and even placed it in my mouth. While I had my finger on the trigger, I considered what taking my life would mean. I felt no real sadness over the end of my existence; that was one of the benefits. I wish I could say that my primary deterrent was the pain my death would cause my family. The thing that really gave me pause was my religious convictions. I had an unshakeable belief that life and death were strictly the providence of God. I had heard enough sermons about the penalty of suicide. While I wasn't certain about the outcome, the risk was too great. I couldn't go through with it. Hence, I trudged on through my gray world, desperate for something I couldn't even identify.

One day as I was driving through a familiar part of town, I felt a strange urge to drive past my church. When the building came into view, the next thought that came was, *I should be in there right now.* The idea seemed a non-sequitur, since I was in no shape to be participating in church activities. I was still smoking weed regularly and floundering in my own depression. Ironically, in spite of my personal failures, which I had managed to conceal from church and family, I had continued to attend church and had been involved in several activities for the past few years.

I resolved at last to call my brother-in-law, Dane. He was a man whose confidence in God was as solid as any I'd ever encountered. We agreed to meet for lunch.

"Hey, brother!" he said, giving me an encouraging grin as we met at a pancake house. We sat down and ordered our lunch. The second our server was out of range, I plunged in.

"How much do you know about my situation over the past few years?"

He looked at me intently. "There have been a few rumors. Why don't you tell me?"

"I'm not going to lie. I've been using alcohol, weed and women. Sometimes other drugs. I've blown a lot of commitments. And I'm still in it."

"What's keeping you there?"

"I'm not sure I can approach God now. I don't think I'm even in the running anymore."

"'In the running?' What's that supposed to mean?"

I related the entire conversation I'd had with Pastor Michaels, the dreadful quote from Hebrews. "I think I'm that guy who walked away from Jesus, and now there's nothing left but judgment for me."

A look of alarm mingled with anger came into his eyes. "That's a lie." He paused, letting that sink in. "Do you really believe the bad things you've done can outweigh what Jesus has done for you?"

"I don't know. How would you interpret that passage?"

Dane's Bible thumped open as he scanned the pages and read the verses from Hebrews aloud. When he was finished he said, "It's a categorical statement. Notice the phrasing, '… if they fall away.' *If.* Do you think God isn't watching? That if you were in danger of going over the precipice, he wouldn't be there to grab you? Here's another scripture from Hebrews: 'Never will I leave you. Never will I forsake you.'"

He had my attention. Dane was flipping the pages a little more. "And here's one from Jude: 'Now all glory to God, who is able to keep you from falling away and will bring you with great joy into his glorious presence without a single fault.'

"If God had really given up on you, we wouldn't be sitting here having this conversation, because none of it would even be bothering you. Jesus died to take the punishment for every bad thing you've ever done. He is with you, and he's not going anywhere. I'm sorry this preacher guy got you so knotted up. What he told you was twisted.

"Honestly, JT, I have sensed God telling me to reach out to you and even encourage you to renew your involvement with the youth group. I trust he has your situation well in hand. Whatever your current failings, he can make all this come out all right. You just have to trust him."

I felt a heavenly charge in Dane's words. For the first time in years, I felt a twinge of excitement when I thought about my future. The person I saw projected in my vision was free from the substance abuse and toxic relationships, a blessing to humanity. But how was I to get there? I was still the man-boy, groping in the dark, controlled by my own base desires and quite afraid to take on the responsibility of life without the crutch of carnal pleasures.

꙳꙳꙳

LOST AND FOUND

Dane had told me about an outreach project with my church that would send us to semi-rural Kentucky to raise buildings at a youth camp for a church there. With only an ethereal nudge to go on, I signed up to go. There were 20 or 30 of us, all teenagers except for a handful of adults to head it up, including me, as impossible as it seemed. I had been entrusted with a position of leadership, actually giving guidance to a group of teens as we went about our work. I looked around at these boys and girls, only a few years younger than me, who were looking up to me! It was both frightening and inspiring.

On a day full of bizarre occurrences, we were in the middle of constructing a pavilion when problems arose with the generator. There was a power surge that took my drill out of commission. The day had already been rife with difficulties. We were behind schedule, and I was losing patience. This fresh setback would require me to drive 50 miles to the nearest Home Depot in order to correct it. I got into the work truck, muttering curses.

I fired the truck up and spewed gravel on my way out, still grumbling. As I turned onto the highway, I reached for the dash to switch the radio on. I turned the knob, but there was nothing but silence. I looked down and checked to be sure the power was on. The radio had worked fine earlier in the day. I hit the radio with the heel of my hand several times and fiddled some more with the knobs. Nothing.

"I can't believe this!" I bellowed at no one. "You've got to be kidding me!"

I could hear nothing but the sound of the truck engine and the tires on the road. I was angry for the first 15 minutes, but as the silence closed in, I felt a growing discomfort. I realized that this was the first time I could remember being alone with my thoughts for more than a minute or two. For years, I had always preferred to have music or television going in the background, even when I wasn't attending directly to it. I had purposely filled my life with activity of any kind.

Suddenly thoughts began to surface in my mind with such clarity and intensity, they were almost audible. The thoughts were questions. All of them.

JT, what are you doing with your life? Who are you living this life for? What are you here to do?

The power in those questions instantly dispelled my petulance over the morning's inconveniences. I began to feel profound misgivings for my choices and a quickening in my spirit. In the core of my being, there was a fresh urgency to cleave to God and leave my own devices behind. There was great excitement in the impulse, but I felt a great dread as well. The residue of my conversation with Pastor Michaels rose up in my mind, bringing with it the whole crushing laundry list of God's expectations. I was finished before I could even start. I began to weep with frustration. But as I drove along, I was reminded of Dane's words to me, and I began to have a strange sort of dialogue with God.

"Look at me. I squandered everything you gave me on cheap pleasures."

Whoever comes to me I will never cast out.

"I sinned with my eyes wide open."

If we confess our sins, he is faithful and just to forgive us our sins and to cleanse us from all unrighteousness.

"You don't understand, Lord. I can't do the Christian life. It's impossible."

For with God nothing shall be impossible.

"I don't have what it takes to walk the walk."

It does not, therefore, depend on man's desire or effort, but on God's mercy.

I began to sense my burdens melting as I talked to God. Now I was shedding tears of relief and joy. I had been bound by so many rules and expectations, but Jesus had set me free. I knew in that moment that all I had to do was trust God.

"I'm yours, Jesus. Have your way in my life!" I cried to God. I laughed aloud as I drove along. Now the silence was savory. The trees and shrubs and horses feeding on the sun-soaked grass — everything in my vision was lovely and pure and heavenly as I rushed by it in the speeding truck. I felt a joy so strong it burned inside me.

‿‿‿

I have no regrets about throwing in my lot with Christ. I have seen astounding coincidences that continue to strengthen my trust in him. One of the first occurred immediately after I returned from Kentucky, unemployed due to a layoff.

GLAD RECRUIT

I had purchased my first house a year before and, under the terms of the loan, was expecting a big check from the IRS. After an entire year, I was still waiting for the check to come. Because I had been in Kentucky for a week, still waiting for the check to arrive, I was in arrears on my mortgage. The bank was on the verge of foreclosing on my house when I got a call from the IRS.

"Mr. King?"

"Yes?"

"This is Phoebe Anderson from the Internal Revenue Service. I'm calling to apologize for the long delay on your first-time-homebuyer bonus check. I'm happy to say that the check was deposited into your bank account this morning. The funds should be available to you immediately. Thank you for your patience."

Not only did the funds arrive at just the right time to avoid foreclosure, I realized that had the check arrived when it was supposed to a year before, I would surely have spent the money on something frivolous.

Still just days within my arrival back in Indiana, I got another call, this one from a friend who had been laid off from the same job as I had.

"JT, this is Fred."

"Hey, Fred. Nice to hear from you. I just got back from Kentucky."

"I know. I'm calling because I got a line on a construction job with Granite Ridge Builders. The recruiter set me up with an interview, and I recommended you as well. Is that okay with you?"

"Are you kidding me?" I couldn't believe it. I went to the interview and landed the gig, which turned out to be the best job I've ever had. I ended up working for them for three years, earning several significant promotions. The job paid extremely well, but the best part was that the owner was a Christian. After I'd been on the payroll for around a year, he pulled me aside.

"JT, you're a good kid." He gave me a wry grin. "I'm glad to have you working for us. I know I can trust you. I also learned that you have been involved in several volunteer efforts with your church. I like to support that kind of thing, so I want you to take whatever time off you need for mission trips and that kind of thing. You just come see me, and it's done."

ॐॐॐ

That's how I found myself swinging a hammer and sweating under the Uganda sun a year and a half later.

"Fred, you're getting eaten alive," I mentioned to my construction partner, with whom I was building an add-on to a church in Kampala. There were insects all over him, but he didn't seem to mind.

"Let 'em eat," Fred said. "They're going to, anyway, and it takes too much time to keep swatting 'em off. Besides, I got every inoculation in the book. Ha!"

With us were half a dozen Kampala locals, who were bringing us fresh lumber, procuring tools and keeping the area spotless. All the while, they went about smiling, white teeth flashing against their brown skin. We had just returned from lunch and a brief conference in the church.

"Wel-be back!" (*welcome back*) called a boy named Julius as he approached the work area. He was sporting a huge grin. Julius is my favorite local. He never utters a complaint, in spite of a painful deformity in his legs.

"I heard a rumor you might start doing missions full time," Fred said, levering some errant nails out of a board.

I stopped my work for a moment. "Who told you that?"

There was the slightest suggestion of a smirk on Fred's face. "I got my sources."

I went back to my work. "Maybe," I admitted, grinning.

"You could do worse," Fred said. "Then again, you'd have to be pretty crazy to sign up for this year round."

I just smiled. *Crazy?* Maybe. *Grateful?* Definitely.

THE VOICE OF FREEDOM
The Story of Abby
Written by Karen Koczwara

Don't tell anyone. You must keep quiet.

His words haunt me as I fight for sleep. Somehow, I know this is all my fault. I must have instigated the circumstances. But I cannot tell a living soul. I must tuck this secret away. I must pretend it has not happened. Even when my mother looks me straight in the eye, I will not spill the truth.

No one will know what he's done.

I will silence it, along with my voice. I will keep smiling for the world, and we will both keep moving on.

૰૰૰

I was born in a small town in Northern Indiana, a sort of blink-and-you-miss-it place with three stoplights and one main street. My family lived on a farm just outside the city limits. Complete with sprawling fields and cattle to chase, it was a young child's paradise.

My twin brother and I were born in the early 1970s, joining two older sisters and a brother. Our home was plenty spacious for our large brood, and though mountains of laundry always littered the yellow shag carpet, no one seemed to mind. There were bigger things to worry about.

LOST AND FOUND

When I was just a year old, my parents divorced. Before I even uttered my first words, my father slipped out of our lives. We visited him a few times, but he eventually disappeared. I was too young to understand the tension in our home, the hurtful words that flew down the hall where my sisters slept. My mother remarried when I was 4, and my stepfather quickly became "Dad." He worked in the agriculture industry, while my mother worked odd shifts at various factory jobs. Though we were not wealthy, we always had a freezer full of meat and a garden full of vegetables to keep our stomachs full. Our broken home seemed mended again, but pain lurked just around the corner.

I spent much of my early years outside, playing with the animals or hanging out in the old barn behind our house. Girl Scouts and 4-H kept me busy during the long, hot summer months. My mother taught me how to cook and sew, but we were not especially close. Her work often left her scrambling at the last minute, and I sometimes felt like an afterthought. I remained a quiet little girl, always obedient but without a lot to say.

When my older sisters were just 16 and 17, they both got pregnant, married and moved out of the house. I was devastated. They had been like second mothers to me, even changing my diapers when I was a baby. Without their company, the house would feel vacant and lonely.

One night, shortly after my sisters moved out, my older brother invited me into his room to watch TV. As we huddled under the covers, the moonlight peeking through the window next to his bed, he whispered quietly, "Do you want to know what people do at night?"

I stared at him, confused, and he proceeded to touch me. At just 8 years old, I didn't know much, but I knew I didn't like it and that it felt wrong. He insisted I not tell anyone — it would be our little secret. Something told me this was not the type of secret giggling little schoolgirls shared behind the bleachers at recess. This was much more serious, and I must never tell.

The abuse continued for the next several years. My parents got a satellite dish with extra channels, and suddenly, a whole new world opened up. My brother introduced me to porn, and the images on the screen blurred with the real-life terror I so desperately tried to erase. I was now a timid little mouse, too afraid to speak up on the playground, in the classroom or at my home. I did not know the depth of my shame and pain that plagued me every single day.

One afternoon, I walked into the kitchen to find my mother standing there. Her eyes darted to me, disapproving and wary. "I found a pair of your underwear in your brother's room," she barked. "Care to explain?"

My heart thudded in my chest. Here was my chance — I could tell her the truth! With just a few words, I could unleash the secret I'd been hiding for so long. But I knew I could not do that.

My brother was good at playing the game, and he had assured me life would not be pleasant if I exposed what he'd done. I took a deep breath and replied as calmly as possible, "I must have dropped them when I was putting away the laundry."

My mother's angry stare disappeared as she nodded and walked away. I breathed a sigh of relief, but inwardly, I wanted to scream. How could my mother not know what was going on under her own roof? Her job was to protect me, yet she'd failed. How could I ever forgive her for that?

Junior high soon arrived, dragging with it the awkward adolescent years. As my body began to blossom, my mother shook her head and sighed. "Now you can get pregnant," she muttered, her mind likely wandering to my sisters' mistakes.

She grew especially protective of me and restricted my activities, putting a damper on my social life. I spent my afternoons in my room, poring over my homework, reading or doing puzzles. All the while, I kept my terrible secret tucked away.

While in our living room one day, my brother approached me as I lounged on the arm of a chair.

"Come here or I'll rape you," he hissed.

"No," I hissed back, defiant. Anger rose in my chest as I stared him down. I was not a little girl anymore. I was stronger, inside and out. I had let him hurt me for four years, but I would not let him lay a finger on me again.

To my surprise, he didn't pursue me further. Not long after that, my brother left for college. Relief swept through me as he packed his things. The home that had become a frightening prison could become a sanctuary again. I would no longer have to worry about him luring me with manipulative threats in the darkness of the night. The budding teenager inside me could finally emerge.

I joined the basketball team in high school and bloomed into an independent young woman. During practice, I discovered I was a good distance runner and decided to take up track and cross-country as well. My coaches and peers took notice, and I received a varsity letter my freshman year. Each day, I ran to school, my feet pounding the road as my house faded into the distance. At last, I was doing what I wanted to do, and no one could rob me of that freedom.

Academics came easily to me as well. When I wasn't playing sports, I hunkered down in my room, dedicated to my homework. I achieved straight As, which I hoped would please my mother, but she still found fault in my grades.

"An A-minus?" my mother muttered, raising her brow as she looked up from my report card one day.

She looked only half serious, but my heart still sank. It seemed that no matter what I did, it wasn't good enough.

I remained a good, quiet kid, always going along with the flow and rarely speaking up. Because I wasn't allowed to participate in anything except sports, I had little opportunity to get into trouble. However, after a game one weekend, I decided to break the rules and stay after to go to the school dance with a boy I liked. After arriving at the dance, my boyfriend ignored me the rest of the night, and I broke up with him. Though disappointed the night had turned into a flop, I was more disappointed that my mother didn't trust me. A chaperoned school dance seemed harmless enough. Why couldn't I have a little fun like the rest of my peers?

I graduated valedictorian of my small class and decided to enroll in college three hours away. After spending my entire life tethered to my home, I was eager to check out the rest of the world. High school had helped me crawl out of my shell, but I knew there was still more to explore. I moved into the dorms and prepared myself for adventure.

The week before classes started, a co-ed invited me to a party. I agreed to attend but made up my mind that I would not drink. I had heard crazy stories of frat and sorority parties and knew they could get pretty wild. My only encounter with alcohol had been a few sips at my cousin's house while sleeping over one night. I had enjoyed the way it made me feel, but because I never got a chance to go out with my peers, I'd never touched it again.

Within a few minutes of arriving at the party, I caved and decided to have a drink. What was the fun of being the only sober kid at a party? Before long, I was wasted. As the music blared, I flitted around the room with ease, laughing and chatting with everyone. For the first time in my life, I felt like I fit in. *So this is what I've been missing out on all this time,* I mused.

I attended a few more parties throughout the semester, and my grades began to plummet. One night, after partying especially hard, I wound up in the hospital on IV fluids after experiencing alcohol poisoning. The incident shook me up, and I decided to focus on school instead of the booze. Though I'd had my douse of fun, I also realized I wasn't being true to myself. I was an athlete and a student, not a social butterfly.

The summer after my freshman year, I took an accounting class at a local college. There, I bumped into a girl named Laura, whom I'd met when playing basketball against her high school team. We'd both played the same position and had guarded each other during the games. She had been a fantastic rival.

"It's good to see you again!" I said, sliding into a seat next to her. "What a small world!"

I also remembered that Laura had a brother named Eric, who had participated in 4-H with me. He was very handsome, and when he walked by, the other girls whispered and giggled under their breath. I had been too shy to pay much attention to him.

One summer evening, I met up with my parents for dinner at a restaurant. To my surprise, Laura was the hostess who ushered us to our seats. As we ate, she sauntered back over to the table and said pleasantly, "Hey, Abby, would you be interested in going out with my brother, Eric?"

I was nearly too stunned to speak. Having not really spent much time with boys in high school, I had no idea what to do on a date. Was it possible the charming Eric was really interested in *me*? The idea was both intimidating and flattering. "Sure, I'll go out with him," I agreed politely.

LOST AND FOUND

When the date night arrived, I grew extremely nervous. I glanced hesitantly at my reflection in the mirror, wondering if I'd gotten my ensemble right. I had no idea what to wear on a date or what purse to carry. *Was I too casual? Too fancy? What if I didn't know what to say or made a fool of myself?* To calm my nerves, I sat down at the piano and played, the music soothing me as I ran my fingers over the keys. First impressions were everything, and I had to make a good one.

Eric was even more handsome than I'd remembered when he arrived at the door. Tall and lean with striking blue eyes and dark, long lashes, he was so good-looking I nearly blushed. He flashed me a genuine smile and drawled, "You look nice."

Relief flooded me at his words. "Thank you," I replied shyly.

We drove to a nearby restaurant and ordered dinner. To my dismay, my sandwich was still frozen when it arrived and tasted horrible. I was so caught up in my conversation with Eric, though, that it hardly mattered. He told me about his livestock operation, which I understood and appreciated, having been in 4-H.

"So, I'm guessing your sister didn't tell you how old I am?" I interjected.

Eric shook his head.

"I'll be 19 in a few weeks."

Eric gazed straight ahead but sputtered, nearly choking on his food. "Oh, wow," he said, trying not to sound too alarmed.

I knew Eric was 22 and going into his senior year of college. I wondered if the age difference would be too much for him and if he'd bother asking me out again. We went to a movie afterward, and to my delight, he reached for my hand as we walked to the car. He called me a few days later to arrange for another date, and I was happy to accept. Prince Charming liked me after all.

I focused on my studies, hoping to finish college with a business degree. I'd decided to pursue accounting with the hopes of landing a good-paying job. Eric and I continued to date more seriously. I learned that after bumping into me in that computer class, his sister had schemed with her mother to set me and Eric up on a date. Eric was extremely goal-oriented and knew what he wanted in a mate. Laura knew I would make a good match. My father had also recognized Eric from the feed store where he worked; Eric had often come in to buy feed for his animals. I was pleased that they hit it off right away, as I knew my father could be an intimidating man.

Shortly after we started dating, I confided in Eric that I'd been abused. "I just want you to know about my past," I told him quietly. Though I'd only known Eric a short time, I knew I could trust him with my heart.

"Thank you for telling me," Eric said kindly after I'd shared my story.

Eric was different than anyone I'd ever met. He had a faith in God and asked me to attend church with him and his family. I didn't know much about God, other than what I'd learned from the handful of times I'd attended church and Vacation Bible School as a kid. Like most people I knew, I believed I was a decent person and would go to heaven when I died. But Eric discussed God like he was a real and present part of his life, and I'd never encountered that before.

I enjoyed going to the little country church with Eric and learning the stories of the Bible as the pastor shared. When they announced an upcoming women's retreat at the church, I decided to squeeze out of my comfort zone and go. I had never done anything like that in my life, and I wanted to find out more about this Jesus everyone kept talking about.

I showed up at the retreat with Eric's sister, not sure what to expect. Several women stood at the front of the room and led us in singing. A few of them started sharing stories of what God had done in their lives, how he had healed them and restored peace in their heart. We then broke into small groups, and other women began to tell their stories. I sat frozen in my seat, my heart thudding as I contemplated sharing my feelings. *What if they judged me or scoffed at my words? What if what I shared wasn't important? What if they raised their eyebrows or laughed at me?*

At last, I cleared my throat, struggling to take a deep breath, and spoke up. "I, um, I guess I never really felt accepted by my family. I never felt good enough for my mother, despite getting straight As in school and being a good athlete. I always felt alienated and alone. But my boyfriend's family has just welcomed me with open arms, and I've actually felt like their daughter and sister since we first started dating. I see something different in them, and I think it's God."

Later that weekend, the leader walked up to me with a kind smile. "Thank you for sharing your story in the small group," she said. "I realize that I've been overly harsh with my daughter, and when I go back home, I want our relationship to be different. It wasn't until you spoke up that I realized I needed to make some changes, so thank you."

I stared at her, incredulous. I had never had anyone approach me with such honesty before. I had half expected her to storm up to me with a few curt words, pointing her finger as my mother had when I was a girl. For the first time in my life, I realized I did have a voice after all. It was small and meek, and sometimes people strained to hear me, but it was still a voice. And that voice, coming from a young, hurt 20-year-old girl, had the power to change someone else's life.

On the last evening of the retreat, I sat in the church sanctuary, crying softly as the women began to sing. Rachel, Eric's oldest sister, glanced over at me, and as our eyes met, we exchanged unspoken words.

"Do you want to go to the front and pray?" her eyes seemed to ask.

I nodded and smiled. She took my hand and gently led me out of the pew and down the aisle. A woman at the front stepped forward to pray with me, and I told her I was ready to make this Jesus everyone else had been talking about a part of my life. I still had much to learn about God and the Bible, but I'd seen enough to realize that I wanted him in my life. As I'd shared with the women in my small group, I saw something different in Eric, Rachel and their family. I witnessed unconditional love, grace and kindness, all things I hadn't known much of growing up. They had an unexplainable peace about them, a glow I believed came straight from their heart. They knew Jesus, and I wanted to know him, too. Rachel didn't know what I had told the woman at the front that evening, but she didn't need to. Her kind eyes and warm, loving embrace said it all. Not only had I been welcomed into their family, but I'd just been welcomed into God's family as well.

Over the next year, I continued to attend church with Eric and grow closer to his family and to God. Slowly, the timid girl who'd hid behind her shyness began to blossom. At last, I realized I had my own identity, and that identity was in Jesus Christ. I had heard the story that God had sent his son, Jesus, to earth to die on a cross, but I had never realized that Jesus had taken the punishment for all the wrong things I'd done, and because of his sacrifice, I could spend eternity with him in heaven. On top of all that, God had sent Jesus to earth to show us how to live. Jesus had modeled humility, kindness, justice and love, all attributes I'd seen Eric's family model as well. Because Jesus loved me for who I was, I did not need to worry about being good enough. I did not need to impress him with straight As or accolades, because he had already accepted me as his own. The idea was wonderfully freeing.

I dove into my Bible, eager to learn from God's written word. Romans 8:28 became one of my favorite verses: "And we know that in all things God works for the good of those who love him, who have been called according to his purpose." Due to my abuse, I'd struggled with poor self-worth and destructive thoughts for much of my life. I could not see how God could ever use such an evil thing for good. But as I continued to read my Bible, I realized that though the abuse itself was not a good thing, God had still used it to draw me into his arms. My years of pain had not been wasted. Instead, they had prepared the path for who I was to become. Despite all I'd endured, God had never abandoned me. And for the first time, I believed that he might use little ol' me to help others someday.

Two days before our first anniversary of dating, Eric invited me to his apartment, where I made lasagna, his favorite meal. "I have dessert," he announced after we'd finished dinner. "Close your eyes, Abby."

His dining room chairs had wheels, and as he spun me around, I braced myself for a pie in the face. *What is he doing? This isn't like him. Eric is always predictable!* I opened my eyes, and to my surprise, they landed on a box of beautiful red roses. I had never received flowers in my life and was thrilled at the gesture.

"Look at the flowers closer," Eric whispered.

I did and saw a green wrapped box with a shiny gold bow. As I pulled it open, Eric knelt to one knee and said softly, "Abby, will you marry me?"

"Yes!" I cried, breathless and overjoyed.

I called my parents with the good news.

"I knew you guys were getting pretty serious and had a hunch he was going to ask you," my father said. "We're really happy for you, Abby."

Our wedding was an unforgettable day of freedom and bliss. My friend from middle school did my hair and makeup, transforming me into a beautiful princess in a white dress. As I stared in the mirror, a huge smile spread to my face. I was no longer shy little Abby, running around the farm in a pair of muddy sneakers chasing cattle. Today, I was a woman, all grown up, about to marry a man I could not wait to spend the rest of my life with.

Unlike on our first date, I was not a bit nervous on our wedding day. As I walked down the aisle toward my groom, my smile grew even wider. After the ceremony, Eric and I made our rounds, dancing and talking with all our friends. At last, I had security. I was safe with Eric, and he would not let me down. Unlike my biological father who had left me years ago, I knew Eric would never stray. I had found a truly good man.

I graduated with a business degree three weeks after we wed and stuck to my plan of pursuing a career in accounting. I'd always loved math and knew it would prove to be a lucrative career. Eric continued with his agriculture business, and we settled into married life. A year into our marriage, I decided to go to counseling. Intimacy with my husband had become difficult, and I knew there was a hole in my heart I needed to heal. I had confided in my pastor about the abuse, but I had never fully dealt with the ramifications of it. I now knew that Jesus loved me and accepted me for who I was. Complete healing was the next step.

I found a good counselor and made an appointment. Over our sessions, I shared with her what my brother had done. As we talked, I realized I had blocked out much of my childhood as a defense mechanism to protect myself. Slowly, the painful memories started to return. I explained to the counselor that I wasn't so much angry at my brother as I was with my mother. In my mind, he'd been just a misguided kid, but my mother had failed to see what was happening under her own roof. The counselor listened attentively and then offered words of validation and encouragement.

"What you are feeling is very real," she confirmed. "You are not alone, and you were not the one who did wrong. You were wronged, and that is very painful. We arc going to work on helping you see your worth. Forgiveness will be part of that process to set you free from your past."

The counselor asked me to name several things I liked about myself. Hesitantly, I named them one by one, and she wrote them down. The exercise was eye-opening for me. Despite earning good grades, being a star athlete, graduating college with a good degree and marrying the man of my dreams, I still struggled with self-worth. I'd never attempted to look for the good in myself because I wasn't sure there was any. Deep down, I'd believed a lie that I was worthless and insignificant. I'd let my mother's disapproval define me. I'd subjected myself to her guilt trips, always feeling I could try harder to please her. But at last, I realized I had value. God loved me, my husband loved me and, at last, *I* could learn to love me, too.

The insight the counselor shared with me aligned with the things I'd been learning at church. She helped me to realize that forgiveness was not about pretending the pain did not occur but about healing my own heart. Withholding forgiveness was like letting a poison slowly seep into my veins. But extending forgiveness meant finding the strength to move forward.

With God's help, I was able to forgive my mother for the hurt she'd caused me. God had forgiven the wrong things I'd done — my sins — when he sent Jesus to die on the cross. He'd sacrificed his only son because he loved us so much. My sister had once confided in me that my father had hit my mother several times, and I now knew that, like me, she bore scars of her own. Through my mother's own pain, she had hurt me. But I was a new person now, and I could see her through God's eyes. With Jesus in my life, I had the opportunity to create a new home with him at the center.

As I continued to heal, I focused on a Bible verse that brought tremendous encouragement. Jeremiah 29:11 reads, "'For I know the plans I have for you,' declares the Lord. 'Plans to prosper you and not to harm you, plans to give you hope and a future.'" Growing up, I had never considered that God had a good plan for my life. But for the first time, I realized that I could trust him completely. He was in control, and though I could not see the big picture, I could follow his lead, trusting that he had my future already mapped out.

I decided to sit my older sister down one day and tell her about the abuse. She had girls of her own now, and I wanted to protect them from my brother. Though he was a grown man and had moved away, I didn't know or trust his intentions. I invited her to a public place, where I hoped I wouldn't have to delve into much detail.

"I think you should know something," I began. "I'm telling you this because I want to protect your girls."

I proceeded to tell my sister about the abuse. Her eyes grew wide, and she listened quietly as I shared. I had never told anyone in my family, but as I'd shared it with a few other trusted people in my life, it had gotten a bit easier to discuss.

"Wow, I had no idea," she whispered when I was done. "I'm so sorry that happened to you, Abby. Thanks for telling me."

Life marched on. Eric, a driven type-A personality, held a successful career in banking. I obtained my CPA license. Though I continued to work in accounting, I stumbled onto a new love. While training other employees, it occurred to me how much I enjoyed explaining things to them and answering their questions. *Perhaps I am suited to be a teacher someday,* I realized. *Maybe I'm not just meant to be an accountant after all!*

LOST AND FOUND

My sister announced her daughter was getting married, and I was thrilled for my niece. She invited my biological father to the wedding. I was unsure how to approach him, as I'd had no contact with him over the years. I'd always considered my mother's second husband my father and had called him "Dad" since I was a little girl. As far as I was concerned, my biological father was nothing but a figment of my past who sent a measly child support check once a month.

As the guests milled around at the wedding reception, my biological father sauntered up to me. *He slightly resembles my twin brother, but he looks nothing like me,* I mused. We made awkward small talk, and I sensed his discomfort. *It's my birthday today, but he has no idea,* I thought sadly. *He knows nothing about my life, actually. He missed it all — the parties, the graduations, the hardship, the milestones. He is nothing but a stranger.*

My husband arrived at my side and sized up the man before me. "Do you even know what today is?" he asked in a steely tone.

My biological father shook his head, his face turning red as he got angry. He launched into a string of excuses, which only made my husband more upset. To my shock, my husband's eyes filled with tears. Always stoic and confident, my husband remained cool and calm in most situations. I had never seen him this upset. He stormed away, and I followed after him.

"I'm sorry I invited him," my sister confessed after the wedding. "I wish I never had. He was being a real jerk."

I was grateful my husband had stood up for me. Because I now had Jesus in my life, I did not let the rejection sink me. God had blessed me with a wonderful stepfather who had watched me grow up and acted as a role model since I was a child. My biological father had chosen another path, but I was not alone. I had a husband who adored me, friends who cared about me and, most importantly, a God who loved me unconditionally. I could not undo the past, but I could make the most of my future. I had a whole life ahead, just waiting to be lived. And though my voice had been squelched for so long, I had slowly found it over the past few years. I was not a timid little girl anymore — I was a woman of value.

Four years into our marriage, I got pregnant with our first child. I gave birth to a beautiful little girl, and Eric and I relished being parents. When she was 3 years old, our son came along, completing our family. Eric embraced fatherhood, diving right in by playing with the kids and taking walks with them. Though we'd been attending his parents' small church, we soon realized it didn't offer much for our children. We tried out another church, and I got involved in their choir. But the environment still didn't seem like the right fit, and we continued to look around for a place to call home.

We learned about County Line Church and decided to give it a try. It was Easter time, and I had just wrapped up singing in the Easter program at the church we'd been attending. The moment we walked into County Line, I was immediately struck by the friendliness of the members. We arrived a bit early and peeked in on a service that was in session. A church member welcomed us and showed us where to take our kids.

"We'd like to go to Sunday school, too," I told him, eager to dive right in.

He seemed pleasantly surprised that we wanted to attend both Sunday school and church. By the end of the morning, we'd made up our minds. One by one, people came up to greet us and welcome us to the church. They were genuine, rather than overbearing, and I quickly envisioned us becoming a part of their family. As we walked out the doors, I knew we would be back.

I got involved with the children's ministry right away and enjoyed working with the kids each week. Once again, I realized how much I loved teaching. Numbers had always been my game, but I had another passion now. Only time would tell how things would unfold. For now, I was content to be a part of County Line Church. Growing up, I'd often felt like an outsider at home and at school. But at County Line, I knew I belonged. I'd found a place where I could be nurtured but also give back. We had finally found our home.

❧❧❧

"Go, team!" The music thudded loudly as the group of cheerleaders kicked up their legs and tossed their pom-poms in the air.

I sat in the stands, watching proudly as my daughter

cheered down below. Attending her games has become a favorite family activity. Now 15, my daughter has blossomed into a beautiful young lady. Our son, 11 and on the brink of adolescence, is ready to join the junior high group at church. The 4-H has become another fun way to bond, bringing back fond memories from my own farming childhood. While my son likes to hunt with my husband, my daughter prefers to spend time with me playing games. On the weekends, we walk down the country road to my in-laws' home nearby, where we enjoy dinner and a few laughs. We are a tight-knit family, always ready for adventure and fun.

For the past five years, I've been working in the classroom, fulfilling my dream of becoming a teacher. Eric has been blessed in his job as well, being promoted to CFO of his company. I maintain a cordial relationship with my brother, though we are not especially close. I've learned to show forgiveness and love to my mother, while setting boundaries at the same time. Life still holds its challenges, but we count our blessings every day.

County Line Church continues to be our home church, and as the years go by, I know there's no place I'd rather be. The pastor's teaching is phenomenal, and each Sunday, I go home with a wealth of knowledge and insight from the Bible.

I still have moments of self-doubt, but when those negative thoughts creep in, I remind myself of all God has done for me. He's healed my heart and taken away the pain that haunted me for so long. He's helped me forgive those who hurt me and equipped me with the courage to develop new friendships. He's helped me to see my value, reminding me that I am a beautiful, priceless piece of gold. And, just like my daughter found her voice cheering on the football field, I've found my voice at last, too. I no longer whisper in the corner, frightened of rejection, afraid to love or be loved. I have discovered the voice of freedom that comes only through Jesus. And no one can ever take that away.

STRENGTH FOR TOMORROW
The Story of Dale Duncan
Written by Karen Koczwara

Cancer.

I hadn't been expecting that ugly word.

Medulloblastoma was the official name of the brain tumor inside my head. It explained the headaches, the tremors, the fainting over the past couple years. At last, I had an answer. But it wasn't a good answer. I knew the statistics, and I'd heard the stories. People died from cancer every single day. Would I be one of them?

There's a 35 or 40 percent chance of survival, the doctor had informed me grimly. That meant there was a 60 percent chance I would not survive.

One question raced through my brain as I digested the somber news. *How will I tell the kids?*

⋙⋙⋙

The year was 1999. I'd been married to my beautiful wife, Dee, for 15 years. Our son, Andrew, was 10 years old, and our daughter, Anna, was just 8. As the owner of a popular golf course in Indiana, I was content with my life. Though I worked long, physically tiring days out in the sun, I was thoroughly satisfied with my job. My children attended a Christian school, our family was involved in church and I served on a local bank board. We had plenty of money to enjoy a comfortable lifestyle. As far as I was concerned, things were nearly perfect. Middle age seemed to be treating me just fine. But things were about to quickly take a turn.

One day, as I picked up a heavy bag of fertilizer on the golf course, a searing pain shot through my head. My head continued to throb, and I feared I might pass out if I did not lay down right then. The headache eventually went away, but it returned a few days later when I hoisted another heavy item over my head. Not long after that, my hands began to shake.

Something must be wrong with me, I thought worriedly.

I went to the doctor and explained my symptoms to him, but he didn't seem terribly concerned.

"Sounds like you just have tremors. It's more common than you think," he told me. "You have a stressful job. Why don't you just try drinking a glass of wine before bed every night?"

I did as he instructed, but my symptoms only worsened. The tremors grew stronger as my hands continued to shake throughout the day. By June 2000, I found myself unable to walk straight, and my speech became slurred when I tried to speak.

"I'm really worried about you," my wife said, her brow furrowing as she watched me struggle. "I think you need to get another opinion."

After doing some research, Dee suggested we try the Mayo Clinic in Rochester, Minnesota. "This place is one of the top-rated medical facilities in the country," she said. "I know it's a few hours away, but I really think you will be in good hands there."

We called and made an appointment with a neurologist for the following week. But my symptoms continue to worsen, and as I stumbled around and struggled with my words, Dee insisted we not wait a day longer. We packed our things and headed to Rochester, eight hours away, praying all the way that we would get some answers soon.

Growing up, life had been fairly idyllic. I was born in the tiny town of Churubusco, Indiana, just a few miles outside the city of Fort Wayne. My father, a hardworking man, was a farmer who also owned an earth-moving business. I was the middle child, sandwiched between an older and younger sister. I spent my early days riding bikes, playing baseball and throwing rocks into the stream near our rural home. I enjoyed playing with my siblings and rarely got into any trouble. My family attended the local Lutheran church, and when I was 12 years old, I asked Jesus to be a part of my heart and life. I knew all the Bible stories, believed in God and wanted him to be real in my life. And from that moment on, he was.

After high school, I attended college and began exploring career options. When the opportunity to buy a local golf course arose, I jumped on it. While very rewarding, the job was demanding as well. I worked from 6 a.m. to 8 p.m. every day, often arriving at work just as the sun started to peek out and going home when it sank into the ground. When winter rolled around and the golf course froze over, I went to visit my sister. It was during one of these times that I met Dee.

While attending church one Sunday, I laid eyes on one of the most beautiful girls I'd ever seen. As we chatted, I became mesmerized with her voice — it was just like an angel's. I learned that Dee had a gift for speaking in other languages and could in fact pick up an accent from wherever she went. She was famous for fooling people into believing she was a native in foreign places. We quickly fell in love, but because my work schedule was so demanding, I did not feel I could give her the proper attention if we married. We dated for the next few years, and Dee remained patiently by my side. At last, in 1984, we exchanged the words we'd long wanted to say: "I do."

I continued to work at the golf course, and we remained active in our church. Dee became pregnant, and we were elated at the idea of parenthood. But the pregnancy ended in miscarriage, and our dreams were shattered. Dee got pregnant again, but she suffered another miscarriage, and our hopes were dashed again.

"I don't want to try anymore," Dee cried, defeated.

"We should try once more," I encouraged her. "Sometimes these things just take time."

We decided to give things another chance, and to our delight, Dee carried the baby to full term. She gave birth to a beautiful little boy in 1989, and two years later, we welcomed a perfect little girl into our home. It seemed our lives were complete. We settled into life as a family of four, never imagining that just a few years later our world would be rocked.

Now, as Dee and I pulled up at the Mayo Clinic, a world of uncertainty lay ahead of us. The place was even more impressive than I'd imagined — beautiful lobby, state-of-the-art equipment and perfectly manicured grounds. I knew there were only three clinics like this in the country, and I considered it a privilege that we'd been able to get an appointment so quickly. But my symptoms were growing worse by the minute, and I didn't know what would happen if we waited much longer.

We stepped into the shiny lobby and approached the front desk. A pleasant woman greeted us and asked if we had an appointment.

"We do, but it's not for another eight days," Dee replied. "But my husband's symptoms are growing worse, and we really need to see someone today."

The woman, whose name badge read Sonya, glanced at her computer. "I'm afraid there's not much I can do. You can't just walk in here and be seen. If you like, I can have you fill out the requisite paperwork, but I can't guarantee you will be seen. The doctors always overbook here."

Dee nodded politely. "That's okay. Thank you. We'll take the paperwork."

We returned to our chairs, and as Dee began to fill out the paperwork, tears spilled down her cheeks. I put my arm around her shoulders and prayed. "God, it is critical that we get in here today. Please work a miracle for us right now."

Dee dried her tears and shuffled back to the front desk to turn the paperwork in. A few minutes later, Sonya called us back up.

"I have an appointment for you right now," she said, a small smile creeping to her lips.

We stared at her in awe. "You do?" I cried.

Sonya shook her head in disbelief. "Yes. The doctor will be able to see you after all. Like I said, they always overbook here. I've never seen anything like that before. Guess today is your lucky day."

Dee and I hugged, thanking God for answering our prayers. A few minutes later, a nurse ushered us back into a room, where a neurologist met with us.

"How were you able to come today?" he asked, looking over my paperwork.

"I don't know," I replied, still dumbfounded.

The neurologist examined me and then performed a biopsy. When he introduced an oncologist, I knew the news couldn't be good.

"You have what's called medulloblastoma," the oncologist informed me as he reviewed my results. "It's a malignant brain tumor that's most often seen in children and rarely in adults."

As he pointed to my scan results, he rattled off several big, unfamiliar words. *Cerebellum. Cerebral hemisphere. Infratentorial primitive neuroectodermal tumor.* But all I heard was one word — cancer.

I didn't know much about cancer. I'd heard stories about people who had suffered with the disease and knew many times it could be fatal. But I'd never imagined it would be me sitting in the chair, receiving a grim diagnosis. Despite my worsening symptoms, I hadn't allowed myself to think of the "c" word. And now here I was, faced with life and death.

The doctor cleared his throat. "If you had waited another 12 hours, there could have been irreversible brain damage. I'm going to give you a steroid for your brain that will help with the swelling, and then we'll work on admitting you for treatment."

Treatment. Of course. I couldn't just hop up and leave. I couldn't make this go away if I tried. It was real, and it was happening to me right now. "What are the odds of survival?" I asked slowly, bracing myself for the worst.

"For someone of your age and condition, I'd say 35 to 40 percent," the doctor replied.

Thirty-five or 40 percent. I swallowed hard. We were not in high school math class discussing equations. We were sitting in a hospital room discussing if I might live. I glanced over at Dee, who sat beside me, her eyes wide as she absorbed the grim news. I knew what she was thinking — *this is worse than we thought. Our worst fears are confirmed.*

Despite the shock of the diagnosis, I remained calm. I knew that God was in control, and his presence comforted me. He had wrapped his arms around us when Dee had miscarried two babies, and he would not leave us now. The situation was big, but God was bigger. And while 35 percent wasn't extremely hopeful, I knew that he could do anything. He had worked a miracle by getting us this much-needed appointment, and he could work another miracle by healing me, if he chose to do that.

If I do die, I will go to heaven. And if I don't, I'll get to take care of my family. The more I thought about it, the more I realized the situation was a win-win. As much as I wanted to remain on earth so I could watch my kids grow up, I also utterly believed that being in God's presence for eternity in heaven would be wonderful. My fate was up to my Creator, and now it was time to trust in him.

The doctors admitted me to the clinic, and Dee and I discussed how we would break the news to our children. She was devastated, and I knew they would be, too. They were old enough to understand something was wrong but too young to fully comprehend such dire circumstances. We prayed, asking God to give us strength in the upcoming days.

"It's going to be okay, no matter what," I assured Dee. "Just keep trusting in God."

As expected, our children took the news very hard. It was difficult to think of them growing up without a father. I wanted the chance to walk my daughter down the aisle when she married someday, and I wanted to be at every one of my son's ball games. Dee was a strong woman, but we made a good team. I prayed God might give me the chance to be a father and a husband for many years to come.

The doctors administered chemotherapy for several days straight. The process was intense and painful, and by the time they were done, I was so weak I could hardly walk. I grew extremely disoriented and stumbled up to my bed, where I fell into a deep sleep. Nearly 30 pounds disappeared from my sturdy 180-pound frame, and as predicted, my hair fell out in chunks. I had always been a fairly athletic guy, able to do 50 push-ups at one time. Now I wondered if I'd ever be able to do a single one again.

After three grueling rounds of chemotherapy, the doctors deemed the procedure too damaging to continue. They decided to stop it and proceed with radiation instead. Every morning when I awoke, I reached for my Bible and read a chapter in the book of Proverbs and three chapters in the book of Psalms. I'd always found the Psalms especially comforting. A guy named David had written the Psalms after running from his enemies and fearing for his life. Much like me, his circumstances remained uncertain and frightening. Though David sometimes questioned God, he also thanked God for staying near to him during that bleak time.

"The Lord is my shepherd, I lack nothing," I read from Psalm 23. "He makes me lie down in green pastures, he leads me beside still waters, he refreshes my soul. He guides me along the right paths for his name's sake. Even though I walk through the darkest valley, I will fear no evil, for you are with me, your rod and staff they comfort me."

God had always been so kind and loving to me. I was in a dark valley, but I was not without hope. I had no reason to stop believing he would take care of me during this difficult time.

Determined to not let my cancer beat me, I decided to stay as active as possible. "Do you think it would hurt me if I tried running up the steps every day?" I asked the oncologist.

He raised his eyebrows, skeptical. "Well, you don't have many red blood cells right now. I'd start slow if you want to try something like that."

I decided to give the exercise an attempt. Between radiation appointments, I ran up and down the stairs at the clinic, trying to tackle a few more every day. *Four more floors. Just four more floors,* I chanted to myself as I struggled to catch my breath. But when weakness overcame me, I dropped to the ground, heaving.

"Are you okay?" the doctors asked, stopping to inspect me as I lay in a heap at the bottom of a flight of stairs.

"Yeah, I'm okay," I assured them, panting hard. I was not ready to give up. I would keep on fighting for my children and my wife.

Dee flew up to Rochester with the kids one week. I'd never been so happy to see them. My daughter came flying toward me, throwing her arms around me and nearly flattening me in her embrace. With all the strength I could muster, I hugged her back. She began to cry, and her tears were contagious. As tears rolled down both of our cheeks, I realized how much I'd missed my family. The days were beginning to feel like years.

Dee became good friends with Sonya, the woman

who'd helped us get our first appointment. Sonya had been quite impressed by the way that appointment had opened up, and she talked about it several times. I knew God had used Sonya to help get me into the Mayo Clinic at that dire hour. The timing had been nothing short of miraculous.

As my treatment continued, the tumor began to shrink. The doctors were surprised and thrilled to see such positive results. I'd sat in my chemotherapy chair between many patients, wondering who would survive and who would not. There was no rhyme or reason to cancer — some people survived, some succumbed to the disease. It was like spinning a wheel and seeing where the marker landed. Whose bed would be empty next? Whose wife would have to say a tearful goodbye? Whose children would go on without a father or mother?

Though the days were often long, I tried not to give in to loneliness or discouragement. Stacks of cards showed up, each of them bearing an encouraging message to get me through the day. I read each of them, thankful for so many friends from church, work and our community. *Get better soon! We're praying for you!* The words sustained me when the night came and the halls grew quiet. I thought of my comfortable bed back home, of Dee sleeping alone between the covers. As wonderful as the clinic had been to me, I was anxious to get back to my family where I belonged.

And then one glorious weekend, the doctors released me to go home for a visit. I was elated to see my family again. My son met me at the door, a baseball glove on his hand.

"Let's throw the ball, Dad!" he called out, a mile-wide smile on his face.

To my delight, I was able to play catch with my son. I thanked God for giving me the strength to toss a ball around the yard again.

We visited our church on Sunday, and it was wonderful to be back.

"Can I ask you something, Dale?" the pastor asked me after the service. "What is your feeling toward God?"

"I feel like I'm in God's favor," I told him with a smile. My response was sincere. I knew many people expected me to be disheartened or even angry at God. But my feelings toward him had never changed. I believed he was in control and that he had planned the number of my days on earth since the beginning of time. Getting upset at God would not do me any good or help me get better. I could only pray and trust in him during this trial. He was the one sustaining me through the good and the bad days. He was the one who'd given me strength to play catch with my son and run up the stairs. And he was the one who would ultimately heal me, if he chose to do that.

On November 15, 2000, just five months after I'd entered the Mayo Clinic, the doctors released me with a clean bill of health. The tumor was completely gone! I called Dee with the good news, and we rejoiced together. I thought of the doctor's grim words not long ago: *35 percent.* I had beaten the odds, but I knew it wasn't about luck. God was the great healer, and he got all the credit for restoring my health.

I returned home, thrilled to be reunited with my family. When faced with the prospect of death, I'd accepted that I'd be in heaven with God if my tumor overcame me. Though I looked forward to being in his presence someday, I was grateful for a second chance at life. I'd have the opportunity to raise my children and watch them grow from adolescents to young adults. I'd be able to return to work at the golf course. And, God willing, I'd be able to do those 50 push-ups again someday soon.

"When I see you, I see a miracle," my pastor told me when I returned to church.

I knew how many folks had been praying for me at church and around our town. Their words and cards had brought comfort to me during my sickness. I was happy to be a part of life again. God was truly good.

৵৵৵

The year was 2011. I'd been cancer free for more than a decade. Though the treatment had killed my pituitary gland, requiring me to take pills for the rest of my life, I was otherwise completely healthy. Slowly, I regained my weight and my strength, and my hair eventually grew back. I got regular scans to ensure the cancer had not returned, and each one came back negative. I thanked God every day for giving me a chance to live and raise my kids. The average person who bumped into me on the street might never guess I'd once been given a slim chance to live.

But now, as I sat in the hospital room with my wife, it was not me receiving a devastating diagnosis — it was Dee.

"I'm afraid your breast cancer has metastasized, and there's nothing more we can do," the doctor said quietly.

Metastasized. I was all too familiar with that word. It wasn't the news we'd hoped to hear. When Dee had first learned she had breast cancer, we'd remained hopeful. Many women beat the disease every year, and we were certain she would be one of them. Dee had always been spunky and full of life. We had no reason to believe she would not make it.

Now, our world was rocked to the core once again as we absorbed the doctor's grim words. It seemed like not long ago I'd been a patient at the Mayo Clinic, struggling to climb up the steps as my treatment weakened me. Now it was Dee's turn, and things weren't looking good. According to the doctor, Dee would never climb a flight of stairs again. I was going to lose my precious wife.

Dee never wavered in her faith during her last days. While on painkillers, she shared the good news of Jesus with a woman in the hospital bed next to her. A smile crept to my lips as I listened to her speak. She told the woman how much Jesus loved her and how the woman could spend eternity in heaven with him if she invited him into her heart. Even at her weakest state, Dee still found the strength to share her faith. It pained me to think about spending the rest of my life without her. But I knew that when she joined those angels in heaven, her beautiful voice would blend right in with theirs.

Dee passed away that year, and I grieved her terribly. I had hoped we'd have many more years together, but as I'd reminded myself when I'd been sick, only God knew the number of our days on earth. Dee would be missed by many.

Several years before, we'd begun attending County Line Church in Auburn. We enjoyed hosting small groups in our home and meeting with other people who loved God. I was grateful for a wonderful church where newcomers were welcomed with open arms. The pastor preached a strong message out of the Bible each week, encouraging everyone to go out and share the good news of Jesus' love. County Line Church was more than just a place to show up to on Sunday mornings — it was a second home.

I continued to run the golf course, grateful for so many wonderful employees who'd worked for me over the years. At 59 years old, I was still young enough to enjoy a few rounds on the green when time permitted. My children, now in their early 20s, were both healthy and happy. As I watched them transform into responsible adults, I thanked God for giving me the chance to watch them grow up. They were truly the light of my life.

God blessed me with a wonderful woman in 2012, and I asked her to marry me. Dee would forever hold a special place in my heart, but I was grateful for a second chance at love. Life had not always been easy, but God had been good. Even when things had seemed bleak, I'd never given up on him. I'd always trusted in his plan, even when I could not see tomorrow. He had worked a miracle and healed me of cancer, amazing even the most skeptical doctors. I had much to be thankful for, and I would never take one single breath for granted.

NEVER GIVE UP
The Story of John Jackson
Written by Arlene Showalter

"Form is everything, son," Grandpa said, turning my body toward him.

"Find your anchor point. Focus on your target."

I followed my grandpa's instructions and let the arrow fly. "Good shot," he said as my arrow found its mark on the paper plate tacked to the bale of straw.

For a boy, ungifted in sports, this was a great boost to my morale, and we spent countless weekends shooting together. Thus began my lifelong love of archery.

స్తాస్తాస్తా

"I don't know how you can do that," Mom said, bending over the table where I was assembling a rattlesnake skeleton, using a magnifying glass to glue the tiny bones together. "You could be an orthopedic surgeon."

Orthopedic surgeon. How sweet those words sounded to ears accustomed to hearing, "John, turn around and pay attention," the mantra of my elementary school teachers. Uplifting words for a boy used to living in the shadow of his straight-A, next-to-perfect, well-behaved older brother.

I took to collecting animal skulls.

"What's that?" Mom asked, pointing to the furry blob dangling from my hand.

"Road kill," I said, grinning.

"Yuck." She shuddered. "What are you going to do with it?"

"Boil the meat off and keep the skull," I said.

"Yuck," she repeated. "Get it out of my kitchen."

In high school, I excelled at the sciences, quite a feat from the boy tested for learning disabilities early on. The heady dream of becoming an orthopedic surgeon, a *somebody*, propelled me to enroll in the pre-med program at Michigan State University, my father's alma mater.

However, in no time, I discovered that partying and girls were far more interesting than studying. Buying pizza, beer and stereo equipment with my student loan money didn't help, either. One night, during my freshman year, I pulled the dorm fire alarm while drunk.

Shortly following this incident, the school sent a letter to my parents stating that my academic performance failed to measure up to their expectations and requested that I leave. I went home to nurse my wounded ego, secretly pleased to be done with the scholastic scene. Working with my hands always came easier to me than book learning.

"We sent your application to Ferris," Dad informed me, referring to my mother's alma mater. "You're going to college. No argument."

"I didn't fill out or sign anything," I protested.

"We did."

NEVER GIVE UP

They dropped me off at Ferris State College in Big Rapids, Michigan, against my will, and I quickly resumed my studies of partying and girls. Before the year ended, I'd given up on obtaining a degree and moved to Traverse City, Michigan, to find my own way. My father and grandfather invested in real estate, and at age 19, I followed suit. I bought my first house, a cozy two-bedroom, one-car garage, with a full basement. Grandpa loaned me the money for the down payment.

I found work installing window treatments for several decorators in the area. I gained experience working for my parents, who owned Horton House Interiors, through high school. I also worked for The Back Room Decorating Center while I attended Ferris.

৵৵৵

"Great party." The cute stranger flashed a brilliant smile. "I'm Victoria, but my friends call me Vicky."

"Thanks," I said. "Glad you're having fun."

"Is this your place?" she asked.

"Sure is."

"It's nice." She picked up my Rubik's Cube, sitting on the coffee table. "I'm addicted to this," she said, laughing.

"So am I."

৵৵৵

"Hey, I remember you," I said to the cashier as I drove through Burger King for a quick lunch. "From my party last month. I enjoyed talking to you. We should get together."

Vicky blushed.

I passed her my phone number, along with the cash for my lunch.

She called.

"Life stinks here," she said.

"Why?"

"I live with my grandparents." She let out a dramatic sigh. "They're so boring."

"I have an idea," I said. "I've got a two-bedroom house. You want to rent the extra room?"

She moved in one day and into my room the next. The extra bedroom remained available, which suited me just fine.

As with what often happens in such arrangements, it wasn't long before Vicky got pregnant. Five months later, we married, but sadness dampened our joy when our first day of marriage was spent at my grandmother's funeral.

Minutes after my son's birth, I raced into the room where friends and family waited.

"Hey, everybody," I said, "it's a boy!"

Every eye stayed focused on the TV. They were showing more interest in what they watched than at my exciting news.

"Shhh!" someone said. "The space shuttle just blew up."

The date: January 28, 1986.

NEVER GIVE UP

We brought Johnny home. My work prospered. Within our first year of marriage, we bought four rental properties and renovated them together.

Life looked good.

A buddy and I took on a $10,000 remodeling job for a single lady. Then he quit, leaving me to side and roof the three-story house alone. *I'll figure it out. Gotta do what I gotta do,* I thought, even though I'd never installed siding before — always willing to tackle new challenges and teaching myself along the way.

After a couple of labor-intensive weeks, I had most of the roof finished when I received a court order in the mail. The lady's nephew had inquired about my qualifications and learned I didn't have a contractor's license.

"The law requires you have a valid contractor's license for any job more than $600 in the state of Michigan," the judge said. "I'm fining you $7,500 as restitution for performing an occupation without a license and placing you on probation. Furthermore, you're prohibited from doing any further remodeling work in this state."

My income dropped from comfortable to zero.

Vicky took a job as a waitress.

I struggled to stay current on my court-ordered restitution payments.

We filed bankruptcy, but I was still obligated to pay restitution.

Hope drained from me like a slow leak, and depression took over.

LOST AND FOUND

Our daycare provider's smooth-talking brother, visiting from Florida, lent a sympathetic ear every time Vicky picked up Johnny. He soon convinced her that life with him promised to be easier and sunnier than sticking with me, a bankrupt contractor. He backed up his smooth talk with smoother action.

Driving around town one night in my 1987 Chevy van, with my toddler son strapped in his car seat, I spotted Smooth-Talker's car at a local motel. I parked across the street and, like a hunter crouched in a deer blind, waited in the brisk November night.

"He sure moved in for the kill," I grumbled. "Got Vicky when she's the most vulnerable."

They came out, eventually, hands glued to each other. I curled my own hands around the 30/30 rifle I had been deer hunting with earlier. "My turn to move in for the kill." They melded for a lingering kiss. *They're so stinking close I could take 'em both out with one shot,* I thought as I peered through the scope.

At that moment something made me glance at my son in the rearview mirror. *I can't do this to Johnny and cause him to lose both his parents in one night.*

As my rage slowly subsided, I took my finger off the trigger, laid the gun beside me and drove quietly away.

Neither knew I'd been there.

I sat alone in our basement a few weeks later, while the TV spewed senseless words and images, drinking from a bottle of Johnny Walker Red Label. I lowered it, studying the label. *Red label. Red ink,* I thought. *We're broke. Losing the house. Winter's coming. Vicky's leaving and taking Johnny. Life is over.*

I grasped the Ithaca Model 37, 12-gauge pump action shotgun that lay across my lap and slowly raised it to my temple. Just before squeezing off the final shot of my life, I called the Third Level Crisis Intervention's hotline.

"Hi," I said, "my wife's leaving me for another guy, and I want to kill them both and set our house on fire. I've got a gun to my head right now." I paused. "I need help."

"Sir," the voice intoned, "obviously you have much more serious problems than we are equipped to deal with over the phone. I'll give you the names and phone numbers of some great counselors. Give one a call in the morning."

I dropped the phone into its cradle, my thumb still resting on the trigger of the gun laid against my head.

Time stopped.

Breathing halted.

I closed my eyes, took aim and squeezed the trigger.

Glass shattered, and smoke filled the room.

Vicky dashed down the stairs.

"What're you doing?" she screamed, gazing at the destroyed TV.

I stared back blankly. Tears slid down her cheeks as she turned and walked back upstairs. I sat in a stupor. *I shot the TV because I had to shoot — something. Why didn't I shoot myself? What stopped me? Who stopped me?*

A strong sensation settled deep in my soul. *Maybe there's a greater purpose for my life and it's not to end here — tonight.* I resolved to live on, counting on nobody but myself.

The next day, Vicky moved out, leaving Johnny behind with me. She returned a few days before Christmas.

Hope soared. *Maybe we can put our family back together.*

I went hunting with a friend on January 1, 1989. While I was gone, Vicky moved out — taking Johnny with her.

Hope died.

On a bitterly cold, windy day in late January, I answered the knock on my door. The sheriff handed me an eviction notice. The attorney, from whom I'd purchased the house, had tricked me into signing the deed back to him because I had no income to pay the winter taxes. I lost my home along with a whole lot of equity.

Depression deepened.

A coworker offered me a place to sleep, stressing it could only be a short while. Paths snaked through his house from all the stuff he owned. Dog hair covered everything.

Will life ever get better?

"Hey, son," my dad said in May. "Your mom and I are going to a two-day seminar/workshop on real estate investing in Chicago. Why don't you come with us?"

"Sure." I agreed because I always enjoyed hearing

motivational speakers, and my morale needed a serious boost.

I met Barb Kalb, one of the speakers at the seminar, who'd been a schoolteacher. She made millions by buying and selling rental properties. We seemed to hit it off, and I asked if I could call her for advice once in a while.

"Of course," she said.

My coworker asked me to move out the following month. *I guess he needed the room for more boxes. Where do I go now?*

Child support and restitution payments sucked up the little money I made, so I spent the next month living in a tent at the local campground. I picked up a couple extra small jobs and found an office, which rented for less than an apartment or house, and slept on the floor. I showered at the nearby marina where my parents docked their boat.

Barb, my new mentor, offered me a job as her "front man" for her real estate seminars in July. A glimmer of hope rose within me.

Could life be turning around?

಄಄಄

That October, while driving past Bethlehem Lutheran Church in Traverse City, I spotted an interesting sign: "Free House — you move."

I dialed the listed number.

"Hello. My name's John Jackson. I'm interested in that free house."

"Great," the receptionist said, giving a deadline to move the structure.

"Hello, Lynn." I called an investor who lived in New Jersey.

"John Jackson here. I work with Barb."

"Hello, John. What's up?"

"I just got a free house that needs to be moved and could use your help," I said.

"What's at stake?"

"You front me the money, and I'll move the house and do all the remodeling work. I'll pay you back when it sells, and we'll split the profit."

"Sounds great. Count me in."

We bought a wooded lot in a nice neighborhood, 12 miles away. I had someone dig a basement. It felt good to have a building project.

Hope increased. Then the neighbors stalled the project, not wanting a dilapidated house to mar their surroundings.

Stress increased. Hope waned.

We got clearance to finish the move. I built a two-car garage and deck, roofed and sided. Inside, I installed new plumbing and refinished the wood floors. I moved in as soon as the building became habitable. It felt good to be living in a house again.

Meanwhile, Vicky had been flitting from Florida to Michigan and back. Around the time I got the free house, she called.

"I'm moving to Florida," she said, "permanently."

"When?"

"Next month."

Her announcement crushed all hope of our getting back together as a family. *Just when things were turning around for me.*

I gotta make this last visit count, I thought, *for 3-year-old Johnny and me.* I drove him to Mackinac Island and hung onto the seat of his pants on the ferry ride, to keep him from taking a dip in Lake Huron.

Autumn leaves blazed from trees and carpeted the streets as Johnny and I took carriage rides around the island. His smiles matched the brilliant fall sunshine, while my heart focused on winter's approaching chill.

Johnny and I returned to Traverse City, where I stayed while he and Vicky moved on to their new lives in sun-washed Florida.

The next year flew by as I worked on the house and did the seminars with Barb. Then her doctor advised her to slow down, ending our work together.

Another disappointment.

જ્જ્જ

About this time I reacquainted myself with Maria, whom I'd met in Chicago at the same seminar where I'd met Barb.

She filled my empty weekends when I drove down to Cleveland to stay with her. Early one morning, as I lay in bed, shouting awakened me. I sprang to my feet and barely got my pants on before her ex-husband, Carlos, burst into the bedroom.

"What are you doing in my house?" Carlos yelled, sticking a pistol in my face.

I struggled to find the words that would keep this guy from killing me.

He and Maria began arguing in their native tongue. Then he slapped the gun against my head.

With my hands in the air, I said, "I'm leaving." I grabbed my clothes and dashed to my car, feeling Carlos' hot breath against my neck. Then I jumped in and slammed the door shut. He kicked the car and spit on it as I peeled away.

I drove to a nearby hospital and called the police.

"I just had a guy put a gun to my head and threaten to kill me," I screamed to the dispatcher and rattled off Maria's address.

I returned to the house after the police left.

"Did they arrest him?" I asked Maria.

"No, Carlos left before they arrived. I told them that nothing happened, and he was only joking around with a water pistol."

I stood there dumbfounded.

"Why did you lie?" I hissed.

"I do not want to see my son's father go to jail."

I left, too. Permanently.

෴෴෴

NEVER GIVE UP

I moved back to Jackson a month later, to help my grandma run her paint store and care for my ailing grandfather. I forfeited my share of the profit on the house because I left before completing the project. Also, moving without informing the court put me in violation of probation.

Michigan issued a statewide warrant for my arrest, but Grandpa wouldn't let anyone else care for him in his final days, except me. I risked arrest for him.

Grandpa passed away in January of 1991.

My folks asked me to hang window treatments at an assisted living facility the following May. Their client, an elderly lady named Ruth, was well known about the place for her sharp tongue and quick temper. I arrived at the appointed date and time, found Ruth's unit and rapped on the door.

"Who is it?"

"John."

"John who?"

"John from Horton House."

The door swung open. "Hello, John from Horton House." I looked her up and down. She was a cute young college girl, grinning at me and wearing a University of Michigan sweatshirt.

"You look good for your age," I sassed, leaning forward. "Is she really as mean as they say?"

She nodded.

Immediately a shrill voice projected from another room.

"Darla," the disembodied voice commanded, "don't you talk to that man, you hear? He's here to work, not visit."

"I'm Ruth's personal assistant," Darla whispered.

"I told you not to talk to that man," Ruth shrieked.

"Just showing him where he needs to hang the drapes," Darla called back, winking at me.

I busied myself with the work order's clipboard, found a scrap of paper and scribbled out a short note. We both worked in silence while notes flitted back and forth like paper butterflies.

Before leaving, I thought, *She's so nice and friendly.* I passed one final note.

I really want to see you again; can I call you?

Darla grinned and grabbed my pencil, writing down her phone number. I called her after she got home. We talked for hours.

"How can you go to University of Michigan?" I groaned. "I attended MSU."

"Don't worry," Darla said. "Actually, I'm going to Anderson University, in Indiana."

I drove back to the assisted living facility the next day. Surprise covered Darla's face when she saw me.

"Can we go out for coffee?" I asked.

We went to Denny's, and after we'd finished our dessert, we wandered the aisles of Meijer's, the only other place open that late in Jackson. I admired her pert ponytail, as bouncy as her personality.

Over the next weeks, as we spent hours on the phone

and hanging out at my family's lake cottage, I started to have feelings for her.

She was different than any other girl and most Christians I'd met. Darla lived her faith. I found myself wanting what she had. Not from anything she said. She knew my story and accepted me for who I was. I respected her commitment to remain a virgin — a rarity in my world.

Even though I'd always believed in God, I never thought myself worthy of being called a Christian. At 16, I went to hang window treatments for some friends of my parents. He was a pastor, but only his wife was home when I got there. Handing me a Bible, she told me I needed to give my life to Christ. So, uh, I did. At least I pretended to. Right there in her kitchen. *Just to get her off my back,* I thought.

In July, less than two months after we first met, I proposed and Darla said yes. She accepted me in spite of my being an older, divorced father to a boy living thousands of miles away. She never judged me for my past. We married on June 20, 1992, a week after Darla's college graduation, and moved into the house we'd bought in Indiana. Over the next two years, I had different jobs, finally settling into a job with a remodeling company.

❧❧❧

Johnny came to Indiana for his annual summer visit in 1993.

"I'm worried about him," I told Darla after Johnny had gone to bed. "He's overweight and not close to where he should be academically for a 7 year old."

"What can you do about it?" she asked.

"I'm concerned enough to fight for custody," I replied.

"That means you'd have to go to Traverse City, doesn't it?"

"Yes, that's where Johnny was born and my divorce was finalized."

"It'll be a big risk," Darla said.

"I know." I stood up, rubbing my hands together. "That restitution is still hanging over my head. I could get arrested for leaving Michigan without paying it off."

"You willing to take that chance?" Darla asked.

"Yes, I am."

"Then I'll back you up," she said, knowing we lacked the funds to pay it off.

The first person to spot me when I walked into the Traverse City courthouse was my probation officer. As my custody hearing was set to begin, two officers came into the courtroom and put me in handcuffs. Darla kept Johnny busy out in the hall so he didn't notice.

This is surreal, I thought. *I'm a wanted man, and my past just caught up with me.*

To make matters worse, my attorney chose that moment to quit, leaving me to defend myself against my ex-wife's experienced lawyer.

For three days, the sheriff allowed me to shower in a private bathroom and change into my suit. Then they'd escort me into the courthouse in handcuffs and remove them just before the elevator doors opened, so my son never had to see me in that condition.

Here I am, sitting in jail again, with my son's future at stake. What am I going to do?

Following a week in jail, my grandmother loaned us the money to pay the remaining balance on the restitution. That was the last time Michigan jailed me. The custody hearing ended with Johnny finishing the fall semester of school in Indiana and then returning to Florida.

శ్రీశ్రీశ్రీ

Two years later we decided to spend a weekend in late August at our family cabins in Atlanta, Michigan, before Johnny returned to Florida. Dad and Mom owned the nicer one, which we dubbed the White Cabin. We called our unfinished one the Brown Cabin.

"Can Landis and I sleep in the Brown Cabin?" Johnny begged, referring to his friend.

"You're only 9."

"We'll be okay," he insisted. "We'll have Charlie sleep with us."

Hearing his name, my dog, Charlie, moved over to Johnny and licked his hand.

"Well," I said, still hesitating, "I suppose you'll be safe with Charlie there to protect you, but …" I paused. "You have to promise not to touch the propane stove."

"We promise," the boys chorused.

"Come on, Charlie!" Johnny shouted as the boys rushed toward the cabin to figure out where to bunk.

Darla and I settled down in the White Cabin with our 4-month-old daughter, Aubrey.

I lay listening to the night noises and babbling creek that separated the two cabins. *It doesn't get better than this,* I thought, as I drifted off to sleep.

Sometime around 2 a.m. Johnny's hysterical screams jolted me awake. I dashed outside. Flames engulfed the Brown Cabin as high as the pine trees surrounding it.

"Quick!" I screamed at both boys. "Bring water from the creek."

Darla jumped in our van and drove to the nearest neighbor, a mile away, and woke them up to call the volunteer fire department. Although nearly blind without her glasses, she drove both ways without them.

Amazingly, Aubrey slept in the cabin through the whole thing.

I heard Charlie yelp from inside. *Ever-present, ever-faithful Charlie.* I plunged into the flames, searching in vain for my buddy and feeling the heat melting my skin. I stumbled back out moments later and staggered into the nearby river, immersing myself in its chilly water, watching helplessly as the cabin burned to the ground within minutes.

"You should have died," the fire captain told me, "because of the toxic gasses and 1,200-degree heat." He looked me over. "You must have someone looking out for you."

"What happened?" I asked Johnny, gritting my teeth against the pain.

"It's my fault," he sobbed. "I killed Charlie."

"How?" Darla asked.

"Dad told me not to touch the propane stove," Johnny choked out, "but I got cold in the night and lit it. I fell asleep. My sleeping bag caught fire." Another sniff. "Charlie woke me up with his barking."

"We tried to get him to come with us," Landis added, "but the more we yelled, the scare-der he got and ran under the table."

"I'm so sorry, Dad," Johnny said.

"It's okay," I said, swallowing back a sob. "I'm glad Charlie saved my son's life."

During the 45-minute ambulance ride to the nearest hospital, I reflected on the events of that evening. *I'm lucky to be alive.* My thoughts traveled back to the time I wanted to take my life. *Now I'm fighting to keep it. Maybe God does have a plan for me; I just don't know what it is.*

The on-call emergency room physician looked me over.

"No more serious than a bad sunburn," he said, emotionlessly, while lathering cream on my burns and bandaging my arms. "Go see your regular doctor Monday." He handed Darla a paper so she'd know what to watch for in case the burns became infected.

We drove back to the remaining cabin, but hours later, blisters developed the size of oranges.

"You have to take me back," I told Darla. "This is no mere sunburn."

"Oh, my God, what happened to you?" the receptionist gasped when we walked into the ER the second time.

"I was here already, a few hours ago."

"Who sent you home?"

Grim-faced, she admitted me with second- and third-degree burns over 40 percent of my body.

"He might not regain full use of his hands," the doctor told Darla as he popped blisters, "but it's too early to tell."

My heart sank. *How will I manage my remodeling and chimney jobs?*

The next day the hospital administrator came by my room. "Don't worry about your bill. Everything is taken care of." This was a blessing, as we had no insurance.

Darla's childhood church took up a collection that covered the hefty ambulance bill.

I spent nine days in the hospital, enduring the excruciating pain of the debridement process. I received heavy doses of morphine and other drugs, experienced hallucinations and vomited often from the medications. Our parents each took a child home with them so Darla could stay with me.

Months of rehab followed upon our return to Anderson, Indiana.

මෙම

"You know what, Darla?" I said, struggling to dress myself with my bandaged hands. "I've been wondering if I can find a way to help make life easier for disabled people."

"How?"

"I don't know. I read an article about voice-activated computers that assist disabled persons in their daily routines."

My interest led me to start V.O.I.C.E. Automation Systems, using a voice-activated computer system that enabled the user to control lights, TV, unlock doors, etc. Although the product worked great, I soon learned that those who needed it couldn't afford to purchase it, and Medicaid didn't typically cover the cost.

My interest in voice-controlled computers continued, and I became a value added reseller for a dental software company, representing both Indiana and Michigan. That led to another job as a sales rep, selling software for auditing medical records.

"I'm so frustrated with this company," I complained to my buddy, Nick.

"What's up?" he asked.

"I'm having a hard time selling this product," I said, "but the prospects keep offering me great tips on how the company could make it more user-friendly."

"So what's the problem?"

"I shared the feedback with the owner, and she just shrugged, saying, 'Too bad. This is the way it is, and we're not changing it.' That doesn't make much sense to me.

You've got to offer people what they want. Do you think we could create our own auditing software?" I asked.

"It doesn't seem that difficult to me," Nick said.

We started working evenings and weekends and developed some great ideas.

I contacted a prior prospect at Indiana Ohio Heart, in Fort Wayne, with my idea.

"Sounds great!" he said. "Get your mockups together, and I'll set up a meeting with my associates on Saturday."

Their enthusiasm spurred me on, but frightened Nick. I pressed forward. He quit.

I scrambled for a replacement programmer. In February of 1998, I launched Technology Solutions, Inc.

My son, Lee, was born on May 14. I sold my first copy of Intelicode Beta the very next day.

In the next months, big dreams hit harsh reality. The new business sucked up all our income. Darla worked as a waitress, and I worked several other jobs.

Doctors lured me with offers of investment capital, which then fizzled. Our financial situation grew worse.

Then my former employer sued me for copyright infringement.

Things looked grim.

I called a high-profile law office in Indianapolis. One of their attorneys, Dean, accepted my case.

"I'd love to help you fight Goliath," he said, scrutinizing my liability insurance policy. He discovered a little-known clause that covered all my legal fees.

NEVER GIVE UP

The case dragged on for a year, finally settling out of court in our favor. My software went on to become number one of its kind in the United States.

In the meantime, Darla and I hung on — barely.

"You're nuts," friends said.

"You need a steady job, a base," my family admonished me. "You're not being fair to Darla or your kids."

Creditors hunted us down, arriving at our house at all hours of the night.

We huddled in the corner of our darkened home, listening to the pounding fists on the front door. We ducked low as a high-beam flashlight stabbed the darkened interior of our home.

"They can only take our stuff. They can't take our kids or what's really important," I whispered to Darla as we all hunkered down together.

Unlike family and friends, Darla's faith in me never faltered.

"We have to pay the phone and Web site first," I said, "for the business."

"I agree," Darla affirmed.

"I'm going to start parking the van down at the hospital," I said. "It can't get repoed; we need it too much."

Money evaporated, while debt expanded.

"I went to my parents for help," Darla said. "Dad sold his tractor to help catch us up on our bills. I knew you wouldn't ask them, so I did. I believe in this business," she continued. "It will prosper someday, but meanwhile, we have to keep things going until we see some income."

My love for Darla grew, but my spirit sagged.

"Foreclosure." Darla handed me the notice.

My heart sank further. *I failed,* I thought. *I can't even provide for my family.*

"You put in a great effort, but you need to know when to say when," friends advised. "What do you know about running a software company, and how do you expect to compete with the 'big boys,' anyway?"

As the sheriff's sale neared, we began looking for another house, back in Michigan. I didn't want to rent and still had dreams of a place with acreage, trees and water.

"I'm going to have to get off here," I said to Darla on the way home to Indiana. The exit read Auburn. "The tire's going low."

While I fixed the tire, Darla thumbed through a real estate magazine she'd grabbed at the gas station.

"Look at this," she said, pointing to a photo. "It's your kind of property — an English Tudor on 10 acres. It just needs TLC."

"There is no way we can afford it," I said, glancing at the ad. "But it can't hurt to look. Let's make an appointment to see it."

"It's in Waterloo," I said after calling the agent. "Just five miles from Auburn."

The house had been vacant several years and was a

wreck. The former owner, who'd lived there 60 years, now lived next door.

It was a beautiful sunny, warm day in November. "This is it," we both said in unison as we ran back to the house after going down to the creek. We couldn't write the offer fast enough.

"There's no money in the account," Darla whispered.

"I know," I said, "but we'll find a way to cover it. We have to."

Giddy on the ride back to Anderson, we brainstormed for ways to cover the check we had written, just in case by some miracle the owners accepted our offer.

That place was *meant* for us, we both felt, in spite of the monumental odds stacked against us. Our car had just been repossessed, our home was going up for sale and we were in the process of being sued by the software company, but we just knew that something or someone was prompting us to take the opportunity.

Amazement and joy lifted our spirits when we learned the owner accepted our offer. We moved in December of 1999, and I set up my office on the upper landing.

Business soared. Then my programmer demanded ownership in my company. When I refused, he stole our entire source code for the software.

I had to start over, from scratch, with a new programmer. Another setback.

A few months after our move, we received a postcard in the mail.

"Look at this," Darla said, waving it like a flag.

"What does it say?" I asked.

"It's the church for you," she said. "It lists all the excuses you use for not going to a church."

"We should check it out."

"You're serious?" Surprise altered Darla's face and voice.

"Yes, I am. This church sounds cool."

Coffee, donuts and friendly smiles met us when we walked into Dayspring. Dr. Phil Chase invited us to join their small group.

The intimate small-group setting helped me to see real Christians living out their faith the same as Darla always had. I observed and learned.

Many of the people in our small group homeschooled their children. After considering it, Darla and I decided we would homeschool Aubrey as well. I was so thankful for this group of friends we'd made. Our time together made such a positive impact on my life.

Meanwhile, Pastor Bill's messages on Sunday mornings began making sense to me.

He emphasized that God saves people by grace alone. I came to understand that grace is God's unmerited favor poured out on us. Even though we didn't deserve it, God sent his son to take the punishment for all the mistakes we've made. He came so that I could be set free. God loved *me* unfailingly, despite all the things I had done. I was a new man.

He often quoted Jeremiah 29:11. "'For I know the

plans I have for you,' declares the Lord, 'plans to prosper you and not to harm you, plans to give you hope and a future.'"

To my own amazement, I found myself enjoying church. I recommitted my life to Christ and was baptized at our annual church picnic.

వావావా

One morning in 2001, Darla and I sat outside, enjoying our morning coffee and looking at the field out back.

"You know what?" I asked her.

"What?"

"I see a pond." I waved a hand. "Right back there."

"That would be nice," she agreed.

I called an expert who looked things over and took soil samples.

"Sorry, but you're not going to have a pond there," he said.

"Why not?"

"All you have here is sand and gravel," he explained, "and you lack proper runoff for a pond that covers a whole acre. It would be cost prohibitive."

Like other times in my life, I could see the end result and knew there had to be a way to do it. I rented a bulldozer and spent a week pushing dirt and shaping the landscape. The pond guy was right — there was a lot of sand and gravel. I had 74 truckloads of clay brought in, rented another dozer to spread it and finished on September 11, 2001.

Darla's brother, Derek, was killed two days later. While planning the funeral, her parents received a letter from Billy Graham, thanking Derek for recommitting his life to Christ — a gift of peace in our sorrow.

Twelve years later, we still sit on our porch, enjoying our morning coffee *and* our pond, filled with crystal clear water, sandy beaches and abundant fish. Our "Faith Pond" provides countless hours of laughter and fun for family and friends.

We paid down our debt and remodeled our home. As our business grew, I undertook my biggest construction project ever — designing and building our new two-story office building.

Both 2006 and 2007 were rollercoaster years. Our daughter, Elaina, was born in April 2006. In November of that year, Darla had a miscarriage, made all the worse because it happened when she was alone with three kids while I was in Texas on a hunting trip.

The loss of our child hit us hard, and the winter months came and went without us stepping foot in church. It was the first time ever that Darla didn't attend church regularly.

Darla began attending a new church regularly in the spring of 2007, and I did not. Our daughter, Natale, was born in November of that year, and our hearts soared. We began to heal from the loss of our child.

రొ రొ రొ

In December 2010, we attended our children's homeschool choir concert at County Line Church of God, and while in the bathroom, I read Pastor Stuart's Dynamic Dad's newsletter.

"I want to try this church," I told Darla on the way home.

"Okay," she agreed, "but only if we go for at least a month."

We met Jen Harris that first Sunday. Her bubbly personality and warm smile gave us an immediate sense of belonging that continues to this day.

I celebrated my 48th birthday, March 4, 2011, with the birth of Lilian, our youngest daughter. Two months later, my grandmother passed away. I had a very close relationship with her and would call her every weekend since my grandfather passed away. I was at her bedside that night.

"God loves you. Do you know that Jesus died for you?" I whispered.

Her eyes affirmed my questions, though she was unable to speak. She drifted away peacefully that night.

In 2010, my love of traditional archery prompted me to start Instinct Archery. In May 2011, my engineer, Matt, and I were developing an arrow quiver when he held up a round piece of foam saying, "Wouldn't it be neat to put this on the end of an arrow and shoot each other?" He designed a blunt to go on the end of an arrow and printed it in our 3D printer. Then we glued the foam onto the blunt. It looked like a giant marshmallow stuck to a Hershey's Kiss.

Archery Tag® was born. We played a game and posted a video on YouTube. Immediately we started getting emails from around the globe from people wanting to know where to play this awesome new sport.

We knew we had stumbled onto something big.

Three months later, I approached Jen Harris, because she was in charge of setting up the Fall Festival at County Line.

"How would you feel about including Archery Tag® in the Fall Festival? It's like dodge ball, but played with bows and arrows."

"It sounds cool! How does it work?" she said, grinning.

"It works on the same principle as paintball," I explained, "but the foam tips make it safer for all ages. Here, let me shoot you."

"Go for it!" Jen said.

I shot her and then I let her shoot me.

"I'm hooked!" she said. "Do you think you could set up a game for the pastoral staff?"

We did, and the staff loved it. We made a video of them playing to advertise the Fall Festival for the congregation. Pastor Stuart Kruse stood up after the video ended and said, "I played it, folks, and it doesn't hurt."

At that moment, an arrow thwacked him in the back. I'd come from behind the choir and tagged him. The people roared with laughter.

How cool is this? I thought. *I just shot my pastor with an arrow in front of the entire congregation and didn't go to jail!*

More than 300 people, of all ages, played Archery Tag® at that festival. It became an instant hit.

In November of 2011, we unveiled Archery Tag® to a worldwide audience at the International Association of Amusement Parks and Attractions show in Orlando. Since then, the popularity of Archery Tag® has gained worldwide interest in many places, including a major theme park in Florida.

ನ್ನ ನ್ನ ನ್ನ

In June 2012, Walt Disney Studios invited Darla and me to take our bows and arrows to Hollywood for the world premiere of Disney's *BRAVE* movie. We celebrated our 20th anniversary by walking down the red carpet, smiling for the cameras along the way. After watching the movie, we spent the rest of the evening helping many celebrities and guests in their formalwear try archery for the first time, using our special foam-tipped arrows — a humbling experience I'll never forget.

ನ್ನ ನ್ನ ನ್ನ

LOST AND FOUND

Success and challenges continue on this journey called life. Spring of 2013 brought explosive growth, but problems with a major supplier forced me to invest a lot of money in new tooling for our Archery Tag® products.

We received our patent for a non-lethal arrow in June of 2013. We now have more than 110 affiliates worldwide in places like Saudi Arabia, Israel, Singapore, Spain and Finland. That same month, Darla and I flew to Ireland, leaving Aubrey there for a summer internship. We set up Archery Tag® on the front lawn of Luttrellstown Castle with 4,000 people in attendance. It was something to behold!

"Form is everything, son," I said to a youngster. "Find your anchor point; focus on your target."

My thoughts drifted back to my grandfather. *He would be so proud to see me passing on his love of archery to people across the globe.*

ॐॐॐ

Flying back from Ireland, I watched the blue skies darken to black as we entered a storm. Our jumbo jetliner began bouncing up and down, like a fishing bob, in the turbulence.

Life is like flying, I thought. *Sometimes the flight is smooth as glass. Other times, like now, we bump along.*

Some folks think Christians enjoy adversity immunity. But, I've struggled and failed. And, I've fought and won.

Am I going to trust that unseen pilot through this

storm? I stare into the blackness. *Trust his training and experience? Or am I going to panic and insist on grabbing the controls myself?*

Outrageous, one may scoff. But this is how we treat our unseen God. We either put our faith in him to get us where we need to go, even in the midst of the storm, or we go back to trusting our own instincts and decisions.

I know people watch me, as a Christian, to see how I handle circumstances. Do I react or respond? React by doing it my way, or respond by turning it over to God — 100 percent?

I'm so thankful that God has been there through it all, in spite of my choices. He continues to guide and amaze me. He's even working on Vicky, my ex-wife, and me, bringing closure and healing after 24 years of pain.

Like the pilot of that plane, God knows the way. I'll never give up. I'll trust my God to lead me home.

HE CARRIED ME
The Story of Marie Miller
Written by Marty Minchin

We had made the appointment with Tyler for the afternoon.

The forecast called for blizzard-like conditions, and as the storm began to blanket our yard in Northeast Indiana with snow, I felt sure he wouldn't come.

Still, we watched out the window. Finally, a single car passed by, blurred a bit by the snowfall. It slowed, then pulled into my mom's driveway next door to turn around.

It's him.

The muffler rumbled as he drove up to our house and eased the car to a stop. When he knocked on the door, my husband, Erv, ushered him inside and led him to our living room, where I waited with our oldest son, Shanan.

"Have a seat." Erv motioned Tyler to a couch.

The silence between this 21-year-old stranger and us sat heavily in the room. I stared at the young man, with his neatly cut hair and shirt tucked into his jeans. Often, I had wondered what he looked like. What he was like. What I possibly would say to him.

We had no idea how to begin a conversation with the person who one day had driven drunk at 11 a.m. and killed my mother and my 16-year-old daughter in a head-on collision.

LOST AND FOUND

Tyler leaned his head down and began to cry, the sobs traveling through his body in waves so great that they made his cowboy boots click together. Soon, Erv, Shanan and I were sobbing, too, creating a wailing chorus that poured out of the bottomless well of hurt inside each of us.

The crying seemed like it would go on forever.

෴෴෴

As a child, I had always dreamed of getting married and raising a family. One of six children, I grew up on a farm in Indiana. My family faithfully attended a Mennonite church nearby. I met Erv at my first job, where he worked in the factory and I worked in the office. I handed out the paychecks every Friday, and that's where I first saw Erv. We started talking at a coworker's wedding reception, and when I was 22 and he was 20, we got married.

My initial plan was to have four or five children, and when Shanan was born in 1977, we thought it was the greatest thing. I gave birth around 9:20 p.m., and when Erv arrived home that night he couldn't wait to share the news with our families. No matter that it was 2 a.m.! He got on the phone to tell them we had a son.

A short 12 months later, I gave birth to our second son, Shaun. Raising two boys so close in age was a joyful but busy time, but I couldn't let go of my desire for a daughter. I had grown up playing with baby dolls, which I loved to dress up. I longed to have my own little girl to dress in ruffles and frills. Unfortunately a doctor had told me that because of a medical condition, I probably wouldn't have any more children. Still, Erv and I joined our young sons in asking God for a daughter to complete our family.

When Shaun started school, I decided to go back to work. Just a few months into my new job, I began to feel poorly. I was pregnant.

When the doctors announced, "It's a girl!" in that hospital room in 1983, I couldn't have been more thrilled. I had planned to name her Shane, keeping with the "Sh" theme in my children's names, but the day before I went to the hospital, Erv told me that he had another idea. He had heard a mother call her daughter "Wendy," and he liked the name.

I loved it. The day she was born, my Shane Lanae became Wendy Janae.

Wendy, it turned out, wasn't interested in girly things. When I put bows in her light blond hair, she ripped them out. She wanted to wear hats like her brothers, who she tromped after around the farm in her boots, helping them feed the pigs. During planting season, she rode on the tractor and the combine with Erv. I had to admit she looked just as cute in her John Deere shirts and blue jeans as she would in a lacy dress.

Wendy was an easy child to raise, a sociable girl with a sweet spirit. She loved her family, her cousins and other children, and she often asked if she could invite her friends over to play. If something was going on, she wanted to be in the middle of it. Our days were filled with family, farm work and long days at the ballparks, where Erv and I coached Little League baseball.

❧❧❧

When Wendy was 12 years old, I noticed that her interest in the Sunday school at our church was growing. She wanted to learn more about God, and I often caught her studying her Sunday school lesson at home. One night she called me into her room, and I was surprised to find her lying on her bed, holding her Bible, with tears running down her face.

"What's wrong?" I asked, sitting down on the bedside next to her.

"God is asking me to invite him into my heart."

Something Wendy heard in church must have triggered her desire to connect with God and form a personal friendship with him. My own heart, which I had long ago dedicated to following God and his teachings, was filled with joy. We cried with the gravity of the moment.

Wendy and I knelt by her bed, and on that quiet night, she, God and I had the most important conversation of her life.

We talked to God together. I helped her find the words for her prayer. Wendy told God she was sorry for all of the things she had done wrong. She asked God to forgive her for anything she had done that broke his laws. I smiled as she told God she wanted to be his friend. God heard Wendy, and that day he connected with her heart in such a way that I knew even her death could not separate them.

❧❧❧

As sociable as Wendy was, the transition into middle school was difficult. Her elementary school had been small, and she saw the friends she had grown up with every day. Several elementary schools fed into the middle school, which was big and overwhelming. She watched kids being bullied and heard cussing and swearing, all of which made her uncomfortable. Wendy stuck it out for a few months before asking me if I would homeschool her.

My initial response was, "No." I had a full-time job. She needed to go to school.

But as the days went by, my heart began to change. I talked to God about it, and the more I thought about homeschooling, the more feasible the idea became. Some of Wendy's friends were homeschooled, why couldn't she do it? My mom lived next door and was always around if Wendy needed help. With a little research I found the A Beka curriculum, which would allow Wendy to watch videos of a teacher in a classroom who occasionally would address "those of you at home." Wendy was an obedient child who always did what she was supposed to do, and I trusted that she could stay home and take charge of her schooling.

She left public school in sixth grade and began

learning at home. After work, I'd often sit down with her for an hour or so to go over her assignments. Sometimes Wendy would take her videos over to Mom's house, and over the years they became very close.

Even though she learned mostly by herself, Wendy kept up with her friends at school. They would get together during the summer for sleepovers or to hang out. By high school, Wendy had joined the church youth group. In late 1999, the societal anxiety over Y2K began to seep into her life, and Wendy wondered why we weren't stockpiling food and necessities like news pundits were instructing people to do.

"God is in control," I would tell her. "He'll watch over us no matter what happens."

Wendy believed me, but I could tell she was still worried. To alleviate her fears, we hosted a New Year's Eve party for her teenage friends at our house to ring in the millennium. When midnight grew near, we gathered them together and prayed as the year 2000 rolled in. In May, Wendy attended a large youth gathering, where she responded to the speaker's invitation to rededicate her life to following God.

 презентет

Wendy finished the homeschool work for her freshman year of high school by early June, and she soon was making plans to visit her cousins, ride her bike to the pool and camp out by our pond with friends. She and her pals from church were organizing community service work in Fort Wayne. In her desk drawer, I later found a stack of invitations and a guest list for a surprise 25th wedding anniversary party for Erv and me that she was planning with my mom. They had already reserved the church basement for the party, which was set for August.

Mom and Wendy loved to shop. They often went to breakfast at a little restaurant five miles up the road and then spent a few hours running errands or browsing through stores. On June 9, I stopped by Wendy's room on my way to work, kissing her goodbye. She was just waking up. I'd never see her again.

Wendy called me later that morning to tell me Mom had asked her to breakfast and that they'd be out shopping for a few hours. We had been invited to several high school graduation parties, and Wendy was going to pick up cards and gifts for the graduates. I imagine they also were going to pick up things for my anniversary party.

I was busy with my job, so I gave Wendy a quick "okay" and hung up. I worked as an administrative assistant in the home health unit at DeKalb Memorial Hospital near Auburn, Indiana, and my office was right next door to the coroner's.

I vaguely remember hearing the sirens of the emergency vehicles as they pulled out that morning, but the sound was so familiar I hardly noticed. The coroner walked out of the building soon afterward. Oftentimes the coroner's secretary would tell us why he was leaving, such as "a little boy drowned," but she wasn't at work on June 9.

The coroner could have been going to a meeting for all I knew.

The call came at 4:30 p.m. It was the pastor of my church.

"There's been a very serious accident." I sat motionless in my office chair.

"Who?"

"Wendy and your mom."

My mind raced as I tried to piece together how my pastor knew about this and I didn't. I worked across the street from the hospital and a few feet away from the coroner.

"Are you in the office alone?"

Many coworkers left the office by 4:30 p.m., but a few were milling about this afternoon.

"There are still people here. How are they? Where are they at?"

I heard the catch in his voice.

"Get a coworker to come into your office with you."

I pulled one of my bosses into the room and pressed the phone back against my ear.

"They're gone."

My pastor's words floated through my head like wispy clouds, not substantial enough for me to absorb them.

"Are you sure? Both of them?"

"I'll be there in a few minutes."

I set the phone down. *Both of them?*

You always hear about this moment. Maybe you have read an article in the newspaper or have watched a televised news report about someone who has experienced an unimaginable tragedy, and you felt so badly. How awful for them. How it could never happen to you.

Both of them?

৵৵৵৵

Wendy and Mom made it to the restaurant for breakfast that morning. A church friend ran into them there and ate with them, reporting later that they both seemed so happy about their plans for the day. They left the restaurant in Mom's Oldsmobile Delta 88. Mom's eyes weren't as sharp as they once were, and now that Wendy had her learner's permit she could drive Mom around. Wendy was scheduled to get her driver's license in three days.

Two miles from the restaurant, on a two-lane road, they were struck head-on by a van coming around a curve. The coroner told me that Wendy tried to swerve out of its way, but she had no time. The impact killed Mom and her instantly.

Tyler lived across the state line in Ohio. He worked nights, and on June 9, a coworker announced that anyone who would help him move that morning could have all the free beer he wanted. Tyler took him up on the offer when he got off the nightshift, and after a morning of loading boxes and drinking beer, he headed home.

He doesn't remember much about the crash. He was tired, it was hot outside and he'd consumed three or four beers. After the crash he pulled himself out of his van and tried to walk, but he couldn't. He crawled over to Mom's car, hoisting himself up to their window. He says he'll never forget what he saw inside. When he closes his eyes, he can still see them.

∂∂∂

I found Erv in a quiet room in the hospital where people were gathering, and we hugged and sobbed. Shanan and Shaun huddled around us, and we hung on to each other as we plunged into a whirlpool of grief. My heart broke when I saw the looks of horror and disbelief etched on my sons' faces. The room grew crowded with coworkers and family, brothers and sisters and nieces and nephews, all crying, asking questions. Why? What happened? Why Wendy and Mom?

After the coroner took Erv aside and told him more details about the crash, there was nothing left to do but go home. Mom had lived in the farmhouse next door to us, and both of our driveways and yards were already packed with cars when we drove in. I tried to smile at the people who were waiting for us at our house, but Erv, the boys and I didn't stop to talk. We silently proceeded to Wendy's room.

A journal was lying open on the floor beside her bed, a pen set on top. Every day, Wendy had written a Bible verse in her journal.

Erv picked up the little book and read, while I sat on

Wendy's bed and cried with Shaun and Shanan. I tried to talk to God. I tried to ask him what was going on, but I couldn't. The words just wouldn't come.

My daughter is gone.

"I can't believe this," Erv finally said.

We looked up at him. He read aloud the verse Wendy had copied from the Bible's book of Psalms for June 8: "I will lie down and sleep in peace for you alone, O Lord, make me dwell in safety."

"I can't believe this, Mom," Shanan whispered.

It seemed as if Wendy had left us a final message, a piece of comfort that floated like a life raft on the vast ocean of our pain. Wendy was safe. She was with God, forever.

ࡘࡘࡘ

The logistical tasks required in matters of death began the next morning. We picked out two caskets and organized a double funeral. Visitors streamed into our house, cleaning, watering flowers and bringing food. But even in the midst of our grief and emotion, none of us could stop thinking about Tyler. Who was he? What did he look like? Why was he driving drunk so early in the day? Was he sorry for what he did?

"Why would anyone do that?" Shanan asked us on a car ride back to our house that night. "How could someone kill two innocent people?"

The coroner told us Tyler had been drinking, and

that's likely why he crossed the centerline. This man, whoever he was, had hurt us in an unimaginable way. However, I knew we couldn't hate him.

"We have to forgive him," I told Shanan. That's as much as I could offer at this point. I didn't want to actually see or get to know this man. But I knew that hating him wouldn't help me recover.

So many people attended the viewing for Wendy and Mom that the last guests didn't start trickling out until around 11 p.m. Endless lines of people had hugged us and told us they were sorry. The emptiness of the room was almost a relief.

As we packed up our things to leave, a family friend approached us with some unsettling news. The young man who killed Wendy and Mom had called the church. He wanted to attend the funeral the next day.

Erv and I stared at him, speechless. With all that had happened, we also might have to deal with looking this man in the face?

"You can say no," Shanan reminded us.

God, I can't do this right now. But I know that someday I will have to meet this man face-to-face.

It might be good for this man to see the funeral and see what he had done and the pain he had caused.

"We need to think about it and pray about it," I told our friend. He nodded in agreement. "We'll let you know in the morning."

As we got in the car, my stomach swam with nausea. Shaun and Shanan were adamant that the man not come to the funeral. They didn't want to see him, and neither did Erv and I.

But I knew there was a solution. The church had prepared for an overflow crowd by setting up a big screen in the basement where the funeral would be projected.

We asked God for guidance. The next morning, we decided that the man could attend the funeral as long as he sat in the basement and did not talk to any of the family. Our friend agreed to relay the message. We added a final note: We would meet with the man, but at a later date. Today, our focus would be on Wendy and Mom.

I wondered during the service whether the man was out there in the crowd of 700 people who came to honor Wendy and Mom.

గాగాగా

That afternoon, we gathered with my family in my mom's garage, winding down and talking about the day's events.

Suddenly, everyone stopped speaking and gaped at the sight outside. The most beautiful double rainbow we had ever seen arced from my house to Mom's house.

It was like Mom and Wendy were telling us that they were home with God and all was well. For one awesome moment, we smiled.

గాగాగా

LOST AND FOUND

Weeks and months passed, and Erv and I began to wonder in earnest who this man was. Our hearts felt uneasy and heavy, compressed by the weight of knowing that God was telling us to reach out to Tyler. We could say that we forgave Tyler for killing Mom and Wendy, but without ever meeting him, it was easy to hold onto a little hatred. Erv and I knew that to be free of what felt like a thousand pounds sitting on our chests, we needed to face this young man and completely forgive him.

Our friend had given us Tyler's phone number, but there was always an excuse not to call. But as time passed, we just felt worse.

One afternoon, I picked up the phone and dialed Tyler's number. I told him who I was and that Erv and I were ready to meet with him. Would he like to get together to talk? He eagerly responded, "Yes." He was ready to come. I could hear the remorse in his voice, and I knew that in his own way, he felt as horrible as we did.

I had invited my family to the meeting, but all of them declined except for one of my sisters, who was disabled and had moved in with us after the crash. A few of them wrote letters to Tyler, but most never spoke to him.

As we sat in the living room with Tyler that afternoon, crying rounds of painful sobs, Shanan finally spoke up.

"I didn't really want to be here tonight, and the only reason I came was to be here and support my mom and dad, but I can see right now that I need to ask you for forgiveness for my feelings toward you." Erv and I echoed Shanan's request.

Tyler's head shot up, and his mouth dropped open. "Are you crazy?"

When he could finally speak in sentences, Tyler had a lot of questions.

"What are you guys doing? Why are you asking me to forgive you? I need to be asking you to forgive me. You have every right to hate me. I don't understand what you're doing."

Tyler rambled on and on, verbally processing his disbelief in Shanan's request. His words shot out between his cries, which seemed never-ending.

"If we don't forgive you, our heavenly father, God, won't forgive us," I explained. "We don't hate you. We don't want to carry around the weight of unforgiveness because it's already tearing us down. The only way for us to find hope after Wendy's death is if we choose to do what's right."

It was clear that Tyler had no idea what that meant. Instead, he offered an explanation of what happened on June 9.

"What's your family like?" I asked when he finished with the details of his story. Tyler told us that he had never had a good relationship with his mother. He had never known his dad, only a rotating circuit of boyfriends coming in and out of his mom's life. His grandparents had stepped in as parents. Did he go to church? Only a few times with his grandparents.

My heart began to forge connections. *This could be my son. My boys weren't always the best, and I know they drank some in high school.* I thought about my own teenage years and my husband's.

But for the grace of God, which has kept us safe, any one of us could have been Tyler.

After two hours of talking, I asked Tyler if we could pray with him. He quickly nodded.

"Let's join hands," I instructed. We stood in a circle, linked by sadness, guilt and the feeling that something amazing was happening as we talked about the tragedy that we shared. I asked Shanan to pray, and as his beautiful words soothed our aching souls, I knew that he, too, was realizing that not too long ago, he could have been Tyler.

"Thank you, God, for the opportunity for us to meet together with Tyler and for safely bringing him to our house. Forgive my family for the feelings we've harbored against Tyler, and please forgive Tyler for what he has done. Help him cope with the tremendous pain he is going through."

Tears squeezed out of our closed eyes as Shanan continued.

"Thank you for what you have brought us through in the past eight months. Help us get through the days, weeks, months and years ahead. Amen."

We hugged the deep hugs of familiarity before Tyler walked back out the front door. He kept shaking his head and telling us that when he had left home that night, he didn't know what would happen when he came to our house. He never expected what took place that night.

Tyler thanked us for inviting him over, and then he was gone.

Erv, Shanan and I looked at each other, a new light in our eyes. The thousand pounds had been lifted from our chests. What an amazing feeling to forgive and to be forgiven. God had set us free from the guilt, bitterness and hatred that could have shackled us into the depths of misery for the rest of our lives.

❧❧❧

Erv and I couldn't stop talking about Tyler's visit. Should we have been bolder and asked him if he had a personal connection with God? It may have been pushing things for our first meeting, but I couldn't let it go.

I wrote Tyler a letter describing the amazing peace that Erv and I had found through offering him forgiveness. If he wanted to know more about Jesus, or even have a friendship with Jesus, he could experience the same peace we had.

You don't have to say big words to talk to God, I wrote. *You just talk to God like you would your wife or your grandpa. Just tell him you're sorry, and ask God to forgive you for the wrong things you have done. It doesn't have to be anything formal. Just pray a simple prayer. Jesus will give you the same peace and love we have.*

I didn't hear from him until the week of his sentencing. Tyler had been charged with operating a vehicle while intoxicated with unlawful blood alcohol content, operating a vehicle while intoxicated while having a previous conviction, two charges of operating a vehicle while intoxicated causing death with a prior conviction and two charges of operating a vehicle causing death.

The night before the sentencing was rough for us. Tyler had decided to plead guilty, so there would be no trial. I felt sorry for Tyler, knowing he was probably going to prison. I wondered how he felt that night.

Around 10:30 p.m., the phone rang. It was Tyler, and he was sobbing.

"I just want to tell you how sorry I am for what I'm going to put you through tomorrow. I know it's going to bring back a lot of memories.

"I want you to know that someday, when I get to heaven, I'm going to tell your mom and your daughter how sorry I am, too. After I read your letter, I talked to God and asked him to forgive me for what I have done. I want to have a friendship with God like you do."

I was thrilled to hear this. No matter what Tyler did in life, he now would live forever in heaven with God.

I still harbored a feeling, however, that Satan didn't want me to truly forgive Tyler. Thoughts would frequently enter my head reminding me of what Tyler had taken from us, and I sensed that an enemy presence was trying to interfere with my forgiveness of Tyler. *Look what he did,* the voice would whisper in my mind. *Look how much you miss your daughter.*

And I did miss Wendy and Mom, every moment.

"We love you, Tyler." I had to push those thoughts out

of my head. "We're praying for you." I hated to think of what he would go through tomorrow.

The prosecuting attorney had asked if I would speak at the sentencing hearing. He believed that the story of our tragedy would be more effective coming from the mother. I had thought a little bit about what I wanted to say. I knew I had to give Tyler credit for the effort he had made to see us, but I didn't want the court to let him off scot-free. In life, I believe, we do have to pay for the things we do wrong. A little time in prison might do Tyler some good.

I climbed into the witness box clutching the few notes I had made to guide my speech. Scanning the courtroom, I recognized many faces of friends and family. When I looked down at the notecard to begin talking, my eyes were so blurred with tears that I couldn't read my writing. I took a deep breath and let my heart speak for me. I knew that our friends from church were praying for me as I spoke.

First, the judge needed to know Wendy and Mom's deaths had left a gap in our lives that would never be filled.

Shanan was getting married that summer, and Wendy loved his fiancée.

"I don't know how we can have a wedding without my daughter and my mom there. Wendy would have been a bridesmaid, and she was so looking forward to it. Family get-togethers aren't right anymore. People are missing. At Christmas, I long for her to be there. Wendy loved to decorate the house for Christmas, and every year Erv would bring home a tree, and Wendy would fill it with lights and ornaments. I don't even want a tree anymore. How can we celebrate Christmas without her?"

The court also needed to know that forgiveness had changed our lives, too. I described our meeting with Tyler at the house.

"I believe that Tyler is truly sorry for what he has done. Tyler told me that he has begun a relationship with God. I believe his life has changed and that he was genuine when he asked for forgiveness from us. When we forgave Tyler and asked him to forgive us for the feelings we harbored about him, we were filled with peace and relief."

I spoke for about 15 minutes. It wasn't until I sat down on the bench that I realized I was still wiping tears from my eyes. The judge nodded to the lawyer, who had a reputation as one of the toughest defense attorneys around, and he stood up to speak. He was so choked up he could hardly form words. I glanced over at the judge, who was wiping his eyes with a tissue.

Truly, God was tangible in that courtroom.

"I have been in this business a long time, and I've never been in a room where I have felt what I feel today," the attorney said. "There's a presence in this room. I don't want it to ever go away."

Sobs echoed around the courtroom.

The judge stood up and called for a 10-minute recess. I didn't look around, but my coworkers told me later that everyone in the room was crying.

Tyler, who had been out on bond and wore street

clothes to the hearing, sat next to his attorney. Tears dripped from his closed eyes; I knew he was talking to God.

The judge sentenced Tyler to two years in prison. Then he was handcuffed and led away.

෫෫෫

That was not the last of Tyler. He began calling us from prison, often at night. He did most of the talking, telling us how he missed his kids and how difficult life was in prison. The other prisoners bullied him and frequently stole his socks and clothing. He told me he couldn't wait for church and Bible study at prison each week. Sometimes he would talk so much that when his allotted 30 minutes were over, the phone would cut off mid-sentence.

Many times, he asked us if we would pray with him over the phone. He said it made him feel so much better. His grandparents were elderly and were only able to visit him a few times, and his wife often couldn't afford to make the trip to the prison.

To be honest, I didn't always feel like talking to Tyler. As the months went on, I just missed Wendy and Mom more, and now I had the boy who had killed them calling me for solace and looking up to Erv and me. At times, he felt like just another weight in my load of grief and my new responsibility of caring for my disabled sister, who had lived with Mom. My strength was running low.

LOST AND FOUND

What are you doing? Look what this guy has done to your life, Satan would murmur in my head. But I always took Tyler's calls. One night I shared what we were going through with some friends from church and told them sometimes our loss and Tyler's growing dependence on us was just too overwhelming. They joined us in praying for Tyler and helped out in providing groceries for his wife and children. We felt a little less alone as these friends began walking shoulder-to-shoulder with us through this ordeal.

Tyler served 10 months of his sentence, and when he got out of prison, he started attending our church. While he was away, his wife had been unable to keep up with the rent on their apartment and had moved in with a relative. With the help of our church, we moved him into the parsonage, a house the church owned for pastors to live in that was currently vacant.

It wasn't always easy seeing Tyler so much over the years. I think it was hard for him, too, because at times he would be absent from church for long stretches. He made an effort, once even inviting us to a cookout at the parsonage.

We got to know his wife and children, and they became part of our church congregation. One Mother's Day, I could sense that Tyler was sitting behind me, but I couldn't keep it together. I lost my composure and began crying during the sermon as memories of Mom and Wendy washed over me. Tyler felt so badly that he walked out of church.

HE CARRIED ME

I told Tyler that I wanted him to move on with his life, and if seeing us brought back too many bad memories, he didn't have to feel obligated to keep in touch. He didn't have to keep sending us cards every Christmas and anniversary of the crash. I knew his life wasn't easy. His wife had gotten pregnant by another man while Tyler was in prison, and Tyler had accepted the child as his own and had two more children with her.

Eventually, Tyler took a new job 50 miles away, and his family moved. I wanted him to go on with his life, and I wanted to go on with mine. If we saw each other, fine; if not, that was okay, too.

Managing my grief from Wendy and Mom's deaths became an ongoing struggle that didn't get easier as the years passed. They were my best friends. We went shopping together every weekend and took trips every year. The pain of Wendy's death was so sharp and immediate that for years I couldn't entertain thoughts of my mom being gone, too. Seven years after the accident, it all came crashing down, and I suffered a nervous breakdown. I wondered where God was. My doctor told me that I was finally accepting their deaths and truly grieving the loss.

God has given me signs, such as the double rainbow right after the crash, that Wendy is okay. Two years after Mom and Wendy died, I dreamed of a group of people, including Wendy, hurrying down beautiful paths and gathering in front of a splendid white gate. They were waiting for it to open. As it slowly swung wide, people poured through it and into the arms of the gathered group. Parents and children, husbands and wives and siblings were joyously reunited.

Wendy stood on her tiptoes, scanning the crowd. No one she knew came through the gate that day, so she walked slowly back down a path by herself.

One morning, that gate in heaven will open, and I will run through it. Wendy and I will see each other again, and I can't fathom the joy of that moment. One day we will be together in heaven, where God says there is no more suffering and death. No more separation.

If someone had told me 20 years ago that I would lose my mother and daughter and then walk through the aftermath with the young man who killed them, I would have replied that I never would have survived the experience. I would have never imagined that I could tell my story in front of a courtroom. But I see now that God carried me through the hardest times, giving me strength and courage when I couldn't muster it on my own. Sometimes God teaches us the most when life is at its lowest point.

Lives have been transformed because of the crash. Tyler and his wife attend church and have relationships with God. Many people have told us that their faith in God has been strengthened as they've watched our story unfold.

౼౼౼

HE CARRIED ME

It was graduation season again, and at a party celebrating our great-niece's graduation, I felt a tap on my shoulder.

"Do you recognize that young lady over there?" my friend asked.

I turned to look at the pretty young woman, who offered a smile and a wave. I had no idea who she was.

"It's Tara," my friend told me. I stared in disbelief. Tyler's stepdaughter had grown up so much that I didn't recognize her!

When I looked at Tara or when I think of Tyler, I don't associate them with the crash. They are friends who we consider Christian brothers and sisters because we share a faith in God.

In the Bible, it states that God separates our wrongdoings from us as far as the east is from the west. That's how I feel about Tyler and his family. If the crash is the east, our friendships are the west. Tyler made bad choices, paid for them and now it's time for us all to move forward.

"How are you?" I asked Tara. "How's your mom?" I hadn't seen them much in the years since they'd moved, but Tara had become friends with my great niece and was here to celebrate. The first time I'd met her, her mom had called one night shortly after Tyler went to prison. They needed groceries and had no money. Erv and I drove to the store right away and bought them food. On the way out of our house that night, I grabbed one of Wendy's baby dolls to give to Tara. She still had it.

LOST AND FOUND

Tara told me that she had graduated from high school the year before and joined the military. She was stationed in Texas and had come home for a visit.

"It's good to see you, Tara," I told her, giving her a hug. And it was.

OPEN HEARTS, OPEN DOORS
The Story of Jen Harris
Written by Karen Koczwara

I'm smarter than this. How could this have happened to someone like me? The doctor's words pounded through my head as I climbed in my car and headed home in a daze.

The road blurred before me as I replayed the diagnosis over and over. STDs were reserved for the overly promiscuous. I'd only casually slept around, and now I'd ruined my life. I'd be nothing but a washed-up girl with no future and no family. No one would want me now.

My anger turned to shame as my heart twisted in my chest. *I must never tell anyone. I'll keep this terrible secret to myself. I'll shut out the world and keep it tucked inside, even if it means being alone forever.*

❧❧❧

In many ways, my early years were idyllic. I was born in 1981 in Garrett, Indiana, where my parents raised my younger brother and me in a modest three-bedroom house. My father and uncle worked together as general contractors, while my mother held a job as a purchaser for a local company. Both my parents were raised in the area, and we were extremely close to our extended family. My cousin, just my age, became like a sister to me from the time we were young. We spent the long, warm summer days telling secrets and happily playing outside.

When I was roughly 5 years old, our family began attending County Line Church. Church and God had always been an important part of our family heritage. My parents had met in Sunday school in their youth, and my grandfather had been a Sunday school teacher for years. I enjoyed attending services as a kid, but outside those church doors, we didn't discuss God every day. Prayers, devotions and Bible readings were saved for Sunday morning when we were all scrubbed down and dressed up.

When I was 12, my parents bought an old farmhouse on a sprawling property just outside town. Built during the Civil War era, the place was dilapidated and in need of a considerable amount of work. One wall of the basement was completely caved in.

"I don't want to live there," I cried to my mother after surveying the mess.

"Just wait till we're done working on it," she promised.

The property became a fun family project as we all dove in, stripping the house down to the studs. As life got busier, church became less of a priority, and as the months slipped by, we stopped going altogether.

That same year, I tasted my first sip of alcohol. My parents were not big drinkers. My father cracked open the occasional beer, and my mom drank a wine cooler here and there. I was a good kid and certainly not looking for trouble, but curiosity and a touch of small-town boredom got the best of me. Two years later, I smoked my first cigarette in my bedroom, making sure to open a window so the smoke would blow out. I liked how relaxed it made me feel, and while I never intended for smoking to become a bad habit, it soon became just that. When some friends offered me a joint not long after, I shrugged my shoulders and gave it a try. The drug made me feel paranoid and panicky, however, and I decided it wasn't for me.

High school rolled around, and I strived to bring home decent grades. I took up FFA, ran track and played the oboe and drums in the school band. Socializing became my priority — I enjoyed making new friends everywhere I went. Though I stayed out of major trouble, I enjoyed the typical weekend party where I knew I could pick up a beer or smoke a few cigarettes. Having a good time was the key, and I always wanted to be at the center of the action.

I got my license, my first job and my first boyfriend before graduating. When I was 17, I entered into a physical relationship with my boyfriend. I liked believing that I was special to someone and convinced myself sex was the way to show love. Deep down, I knew from the way I'd been raised that premarital sex was wrong, but I tried to justify my actions in my head. *It's everywhere I go — on TV, in the movies, in the magazines, on the billboards, too. Everyone seems to be doing it, so what's the big deal?*

Immediately following graduation, I moved out of my house and began general education classes at a college in Fort Wayne, 20 minutes away. I had no idea what I wanted to do with the rest of my life or what sort of career to pursue. Instead of focusing on my studies, I began skipping classes and dove into the party scene. Booze and boys became the center of my world as I sought out a good time every chance I got. With a couple beers in my system, I became a happy drunk. School slid down the priority ladder as my grades plummeted. I kept up a full-time job but incurred significant credit card debt. Life became a blur of parties and hangovers as I struggled to stay afloat.

One day, shortly after completing my freshman year, I received a letter in the mail from the college admissions office. The college had put me on academic probation due to my poor grades. I was required to sit out one semester before returning to classes on campus again.

I decided to put my efforts into my work instead and got a full-time job as a manager in the floral department at a local grocery store. I tried to return to college the following year but did not receive any scholarships or financial aid, forcing me to work even harder to pay my bills. Eventually, burnt out by the responsibility, I dropped out of college and focused on work. I became a department manager at a home improvement store and enjoyed the job. The money was decent, as were the benefits. *I'll just stick with this for now,* I decided.

On the weekends, I hit the bars, looking for a chance to spice up the mundane weekdays. After throwing back a few beers, I made my rounds, chatting with the locals and flirting with guys. The dim lights, clanging glasses, smoky air and cacophony of voices over the thumping music became a regular scene. I began dating a new guy, and within a short time, we slept together. Sex had now become a casual thing to me. *This is just what young people do,* I reminded myself. *You're not normal if you're a 20-something-year-old not having sex.*

My Aunt Debbie called me one Sunday morning to invite me to church. "Would you like to go with me?" she asked pleasantly.

"Oh, thanks, but not this morning. I'm pretty tired from working all week," I replied groggily, rubbing the sleep from my eyes.

As I rolled out of bed, I caught a glimpse of myself in the mirror. My clothes were rumpled and still reeked of smoke, and my bloodshot eyes were a telltale sign I'd had a few too many drinks the night before. In truth, I had a hangover, but I didn't want to tell Aunt Debbie that. I loved her and was grateful she cared enough to think of me. But church wasn't on my radar anymore. I had better things to do. Maybe I'd get around to it someday down the road.

I discovered the guy I'd been dating had another girlfriend. She approached me with some bad news. "He gave me HPV. I just want to let you know in case he passed it on to you," she told me regretfully.

My chest tightened. I'd heard of HPV — Human Papillomavirus — before, and I knew it was a highly contagious sexually transmitted virus. I went to the doctor and tested for it, but the results came back negative. I breathed a sigh of relief, thankful to be off the hook. But a few months later, my luck ran out, and my world was rocked to the core.

"I'm sorry to inform you that your test came back positive," the doctor told me. "You have HPV."

My heart sank to the floor as I sat frozen in my chair. I was only 24 years old with a whole life ahead of me. *How could this have happened? I am smarter than that,* I chided myself angrily. I'd used protection and didn't consider myself overly promiscuous. What was I going to do now?

As soon as I left the doctor's office, I called my cousin, with whom I shared an apartment at the time. "I need to tell you something," I began quietly. I told her about the diagnosis and how embarrassed I was.

"You are going to be okay," she assured me kindly.

I wasn't so sure, however. I was a good girl from a decent home. These sorts of things didn't happen to good girls.

I had made a real mess of things.

As the days passed, I grew more depressed. Though HPV was one of the more common viruses, I knew there was a huge stigma wrapped around STDs. *Who will want me now?* I thought sadly. *I might not ever be able to have children. I'm all washed up now. I've ruined my life.*

I'd been casually dating a guy, but our relationship soon dissolved. I poured myself into my work and kept the shameful secret to myself. *I'm done dating,* I decided adamantly. *If anyone finds out about the virus, he surely won't want anything to do with me. Better to stay away from guys for now.*

But the secret weighed heavily on me. Eventually, I decided to throw myself back into the dating world. I met a new guy, and within a few months, we grew serious. I confided in him about the HPV diagnosis, and he remained supportive. But not long after I opened up to him, he turned his back on me. He showed up at my friends' workplaces and asked them if I'd been seeing anyone else. He then went straight to my parents and revealed my shameful secret. I was mortified when I discovered what he'd done.

"Your boyfriend says you have HPV," my mother said worriedly. "I don't even know what that is, Jennifer. Is it serious?"

I took a deep breath. "It's a sexually transmitted virus," I explained, embarrassed to be discussing such details with my parents. "It's pretty common. I guess I was just one of the unlucky ones who caught it."

My father nodded, his face solemn but forgiving. "We love you, Jennifer, and we support you. We may not agree with the lifestyle you're living, but we don't love you any less right now than we have in the past."

I was grateful for their support but still ashamed and angry. I had confided in my boyfriend, and he had betrayed me. How could I ever trust anyone again? I hunkered down into hermit mode, convinced I would just spend the rest of my life working hard and remaining alone.

I am done with relationships. I don't want to risk ruining anyone else's life.

A deep depression sank in as the months dragged by. I got an apartment of my own and went through the motions of everyday life. Each morning, I headed off to work, where I put on a smile for my customers, all the while hiding my shame and pain. In the evenings, I walked the dog and took care of the necessary chores, but I put my social life on hold. As far as I was concerned, I was a pariah, unworthy of any real relationship. Life took on a mundane pace, and I accepted it as the new normal.

I returned to the doctor several times and had him re-test me, hoping perhaps the virus had disappeared. But he had disheartening news.

"Honey, I know what you're trying to do," he told me soberly. "But it's not going away on its own. HPV remains in your system for the rest of your life. You have two of the worst strains of the virus. It never fully disappears."

Never goes away. My heart sank. Somehow, deep down, I had known this. But his words sounded so grim and final, like a death sentence of sorts. After doing some research, I learned that though many people were affected by HPV and lived perfectly normal lives, a few were not so fortunate. HPV could turn into cervical cancer in certain patients. The idea of getting cancer or passing the virus on to someone else was unthinkable. I wished I could take back all my choices, but it was too late.

"Let me guess. You don't know anyone with this, do you?" the doctor said gently.

I shook my head, filled with shame. "No."

"I know, no one talks about this stuff. If only you knew how many cases of HPV I deal with every single day. I've already seen five cases this morning."

I stared at him in disbelief. "You're kidding."

"Nope. If you're sexually active, you're very likely to have it. It's much more common than you think."

His words relieved me. Since my diagnosis, I had walked around feeling as if I was the only one in the world with the virus. Embarrassed, I'd wondered if anyone would ever love me despite my shameful secret. It was good to know I was not alone.

One Saturday afternoon, as my aunt and I stood together in my grandmother's kitchen, she turned to me with a wide smile. "Jenny, you're going to church with me tomorrow morning." It was more of a command than a suggestion. I was depressed and lonely and figured it couldn't hurt to get out and be around other people. Plus, maybe I'd learn a thing or two.

"Okay, I'll go," I agreed.

My nerves rattled me a bit as I pulled up at County Line Church. Judging from the hundreds of cars in the parking lot, it looked as though the church had grown quite a bit since I'd last been there. I took a deep breath and walked through the doors. To my surprise, I saw many familiar faces.

"Hey, good to see you, Jen!" a few folks called out, smiling at me.

I smiled back, thankful for the warm welcome after being away for so many years. As I took a seat for the service and glanced around, I realized how much I'd missed being here. There was something comforting about returning to a place so familiar, like walking into a grandmother's house and finding a hot apple pie waiting on the table. *This is nice,* I told myself. *It feels like home. I need to start coming again.*

Two weeks later, rumors of financial trouble began flying around the store where I worked. I knew things weren't great, but I didn't think they were as bad as some said. I brushed off the rumors and focused on my work, grateful for the friendships with my coworkers and the busy schedule that kept my mind off my woes.

Within a matter of weeks, however, things at work took a drastic turn for the worse. Several of our other stores abruptly closed, and the area manager informed us ours would be closing as well. Most of our employees were laid off, leaving just me and two other coworkers at our location.

"We're going to need to liquidate all assets," the manager informed us. "You need to get the store ready for auction."

Just like that, my world was rocked once again. I went from a thriving manager of a successful home improvement store to a girl scrambling to stay afloat. We never received an explanation for the rapid turn of events. Instead, we were forced to jump into action and get rid of everything as quickly as possible. As soon as our doors closed, I'd be left without a job. With little money in my bank account, I'd find myself on the streets if I didn't secure other employment soon.

"We have all these custom-made doors and other orders," I told my manager. "Our customers are going to be coming to pick them up. What am I supposed to tell them?"

"Legally, we can't give them their product, even though they've already paid for it," the manager replied grimly. "All of those orders are now considered property of the store bankruptcy. If we hand it over, we could be held in contempt of court."

Contempt of court? I felt sick to my stomach at the idea of my hardworking, loyal customers not being able to pick up their product. *This isn't right. How can this be happening?* I wondered in disbelief.

The final days of the store's business loomed. As I climbed out of bed, my legs felt like lead, and each step toward my car was filled with dread. How could I break this bad news to my customers? Surely, they would be furious and rightfully so! Things were going to get ugly, I was sure of it. On top of that mess, I was about to be out of a job and had not one prospect in sight. I was only 25 years old, yet I felt decades older, as if the whole world had been dumped on my shoulders overnight. What was I going to do now?

As I drove to work, I decided to stop off at my favorite coffee shop, Brewdaily, for my requisite iced latte. Perhaps a little coffee would help ease my anxiety. As I walked into the shop, I spotted the senior pastor of County Line Church. Seated at a little table, he appeared to be having a meeting. *I doubt he recognizes me,* I thought as I inched my way through the line. *After all, I've only been going back to the church for the past couple weeks, and there are at least 700 to 800 people there.*

But to my surprise, the pastor glanced up and smiled at me. "Hi, Jen! Having a good morning?!" he called out.

I looked at him in disbelief. *He knows me?* And then, before I could stop myself, the dam inside me burst, and tears began to spill down my cheeks.

"Sit down here. What's the matter?" The pastor patted the chair next to him, his eyes warm and sympathetic.

I sank into the chair and opened up to him, sharing everything that had been going on at my work. "I just feel terrible," I confessed. "I feel like I've personally betrayed all these people."

"Do you mind if I pray for you?" he asked gently.

I shook my head. "No, that would be great."

The pastor prayed, asking God to give me peace and confidence as I went to my work and broke the bad news. Until I'd started going back to church with my aunt, I hadn't given much thought to God in quite a long time. I wasn't quite sure how to pray to him or if he even listened to my prayers anymore. I'd made plenty of bad choices over the past few years. Was it possible he still wanted anything to do with me?

I thanked the pastor and returned to my car, taking a long sip of my latte. As I headed down the road, I began to cry again, my tears making it difficult to see out the window. "God, if you are who you say you are, I need to know that you are real. I just need to know that right now — are you real?" The pastor at the coffee shop talked to God like he was real, but I still wasn't convinced. What if he was just some far-off guy in the sky who didn't care about our problems down here on earth? Was God really in the details of store bankruptcies and financial troubles?

Suddenly, clear as if he was talking out loud, I heard God say to me, "I am who I say I am. I have always been here. No one walked away but you."

A chill ran down my spine as the words echoed in my head. I knew without a doubt I'd just heard God speak to me. And for the first time in my life, I fully believed in my heart that he was real. A light came on in that moment as the tears continued to spill down my cheeks.

No one walked away but you. I had accepted Jesus into my heart when I was a young kid, praying along with my Sunday school teacher at church. I believed that God had sent his son, Jesus, to earth to die on the cross for the wrong things we'd done, and I'd prayed because I wanted to spend eternity in heaven with him. But beyond that prayer, I hadn't done much with my faith. God, church and the Bible had all become like a fond memory of a trip taken years ago — it had been nice, but I hadn't visited since.

Today, however, driving to work, at the end of myself, I discovered something I hadn't felt in a long time — hope. God had never moved. He had never abandoned me. He had always remained the same. It was me who had given up on him. When I'd set church by the wayside years ago, I'd filled my life with busyness, focusing on school, boys and partying. I'd tried to find purpose and fulfillment in bars, hoping intimate relationships would ease my loneliness. But in the end, none of that had brought true happiness. Now, on the brink of unemployment, I faced my toughest battle yet. But I wasn't about to face it alone. I had God by my side, and he would help me get through this difficult time.

With God's help, I faced my customers with dignity and grace. Afraid I'd be unable to afford rent at my current place, I moved into an apartment my father and uncle owned. Just before our store closed its doors, a couple came in. I recognized them as regulars at the coffee shop I frequented often.

After I explained we were closing and I'd soon be out of a job, the woman said to me, "Hey, you used to be a florist, didn't you?"

I nodded.

"I could use someone in my floral shop. Would you be interested in working there?"

"Yeah, that might work out great," I agreed enthusiastically.

Two weeks after our store closed down for good, I started work at the floral shop. The woman's husband owned a printing company and offered me part-time work as an outside sales representative as well. I was happy to be able to pay my bills once again. All my worries of being unemployed dissipated as I thanked God for providing for my needs.

As the months marched by, I dusted off my Bible and began thumbing through, poring over the stories and verses between the pages. I found the reading interesting, and I began talking with God, trying to get to know him better. On Sundays, I attended County Line Church. I enjoyed hearing the pastor's encouraging message and was impressed by the friendliness of the members. Though I had walked away from the church for years, it was as if I had never left. Everyone welcomed me with open arms, and for the first time in a long while, I didn't feel so lonely.

When Friday night rolled around, however, I still hit up the bars. I liked to have a good time and never wanted to miss out on the fun. As I threw back a few shots and downed a couple beers, I mingled with the crowd, figuring there was no harm in a little drunken festivity. Drinking was a nice way to escape. For a few hours, I didn't have to think about the idea that I carried around an incurable virus that could affect the rest of my life.

I kept up this pattern for a while, working, attending church and making my rounds at the bars on the weekends. But something was shifting inside of me. I was genuinely interested in God, and I knew that he cared for me. From my meeting with the pastor at the coffee shop to the couple who'd offered me a job when I was at my end, I had seen God clearly intervene in my life. He had believed in me even when I'd been unsure about him. He was the great healer, the great comforter and a true friend. As I started to pray and talk to him, I slowly began to trust him. The Bible states that God forgives all of our past mistakes if we simply ask him to cleanse us. By doing just that, I could be set free. I didn't need to beat myself up for my past, because he'd already washed it all away. I'd sung songs about God's love and forgiveness at County Line Church as a kid, but now, as a grown woman returning to that same church, it was finally time to believe those truths.

Two years after my store closed, my cousins invited me over to watch the Colts play in the Super Bowl. They were all huge football fans, and I was happy to spend time with them and watch the game. Not long after I arrived at the house, a cute guy I recognized showed up. I'd met him at a wedding, and he'd gone fishing with my family before. Zack and I chatted and hit it off that Sunday afternoon, but I didn't think much of the encounter, as I was dating someone at the time.

Three months later, I broke up with the guy I'd been seeing, and my cousin gave Zack my phone number. He called and asked me out. We went to dinner and a movie and had a great time. The following night, he came over to my parents' house for a card tournament. We were inseparable from then on. Like me, he enjoyed anything outdoors — fishing, canoeing, camping and hunting. On top of having lots in common with me, he was funny, sweet, sincere and very cute. My family approved of our relationship and even joked that they'd acted as a dating service by setting us up.

OPEN HEARTS, OPEN DOORS

My boyfriend remained very respectful of physical boundaries. Two months into our relationship, I decided to open up to him and share the secret I'd kept from most of the world.

"I have HPV," I told him quietly one night, tears filling my eyes as I stared at the floor in shame. Though this man had proven he loved me just as I was, I'd still held on to the stigma of my condition.

He looked straight at me and smiled. "Listen, it is what it is. It's not a big deal. I can't help who I'm falling in love with."

Relief swept through me at his kind words. "Really?" I sniffed. I'd spent so long wondering if anyone would love me just as I was, and finally I had met that man.

We dated through the summer and grew more serious the more time we spent together. One day, my coworker at the floral shop sent me on a special delivery. "I need you to go deliver these flowers to this botanical conservatory in Fort Wayne," she instructed.

I raised my brow skeptically. "Fort Wayne?" Our shop was a few minutes outside of the city, and we rarely delivered arrangements there. "Okay, well, I'll be off."

When I arrived at the conservatory, I walked into a beautiful tropical room, complete with colorful foliage and a cascading waterfall. There, under that waterfall, stood my boyfriend, grinning from ear to ear.

I gasped. "What are you doing here?"

"Those flowers are for you," he said, nodding toward the gorgeous bouquet in my hand. "Open up the card."

LOST AND FOUND

I did, my heart racing as I slid the card out of the envelope. "Jen, I love you. Will you marry me?" it read.

"Yes!" I gushed, racing to throw my arms around him.

We began planning for a June wedding the following year. Meanwhile, we got more involved at County Line Church, serving on the hospitality team together on the weekends. Pastor Bob walked us through premarital counseling, and I was grateful for his insight as we neared our wedding day. I was also grateful that I'd met such a wonderful guy who loved me, loved God and was open to serving other people. The more time I spent at church, the more I realized I had no need for the bars anymore. They offered shallow, temporary fun, but at church, I'd found meaningful, lasting relationships. I would always be a social butterfly, but now I had a healthy place to pursue friendships.

We married in a beautiful ceremony at the church that June. The flower arrangements — beautiful hues of pink, apricot and sage green — came straight from the floral shop where I worked. Zack's groomsmen wore fishing flies on their boutonnieres in honor of our favorite hobby, fly fishing. As we stood before our friends and family, Pastor Bob shared a few words of wisdom.

"I'm going to leave you with this acronym: O.N.E. It stands for Open Communication, New Priorities and Exalt Christ in your relationship. Just remember those three important things when life gets tough, and you'll be okay."

Not long after we wed, I discovered I was pregnant. I

was both elated and terrified. I knew pregnancy could complicate my HPV. What if I transmitted the virus to the baby? How could I deal with that trauma?

I prayed and read my Bible, focusing on the verse Philippians 4:6-7: "Do not be anxious about anything, but in every situation, by prayer and petition, with thanksgiving, present your requests to God. And the peace of God, which transcends all understanding, will guard your hearts and your minds in Christ Jesus." Being anxious wouldn't do me any good. I needed to release my fears to God and trust that he would take care of the child growing inside of me.

I gave birth to a little girl we named Ryann. After she uttered her first cry, the doctors ushered her off to be examined. Much to my relief and joy, they announced her perfectly healthy. I cried tears of happiness, thanking God that he had entrusted me with the most beautiful, cherished gift on earth. All my fears had been unmerited. I had a healthy baby girl.

My doctor had me come back for an exam when my daughter was 6 weeks old. "The good news is your HPV isn't pre-cancerous, but it is active and moving," the doctor informed me.

I broke down bawling, devastated at the news.

"Look, you can keep having babies. I'll deliver one baby, I'll deliver 10 babies of yours. But with each pregnancy, your immune system does drop. You are playing Russian Roulette every time you get pregnant. And with each pregnancy, that could be the one where I tell you that your HPV has turned into full-blown cervical cancer," the doctor explained.

I nodded solemnly. "I understand."

My husband and I discussed our options. We were in love with our baby girl and knew we'd like to have at least one more child. I was still young and otherwise very healthy. I decided to take a chance, and just a few months after giving birth to our daughter, I got pregnant again. God had given me one healthy baby, and I trusted that he would give me another one. I tried not to let my fears hinder my excitement as my belly began to grow again.

Though I'd worked most of my adult life, I decided that when I had my second baby, I'd stay home with the children. One Sunday morning, however, the pastor announced they were looking for someone to fill a position as the church hospitality and communications director. As I sat in the pew, I turned to my husband, and he stared back at me, his eyes meeting mine.

"That's a neat job," I whispered.

"You would be perfect at that," he whispered back.

I smiled. "I would love that job."

"You should try for it," he encouraged me.

"Oh, I don't have the qualifications for that," I told him, dismissing it.

But I could not stop thinking about the position. I loved people, I loved my church and I'd already been volunteering at the welcome center for some time. Deep down, I believed my husband was right. It would be a perfect job for me. I decided to apply, and to my pleasant surprise, I snagged an interview. A few days later, to my even greater surprise, the church offered me the position. Though I'd intended on staying home with my kids, the position was too great to pass up. I knew it was a gift straight from God.

The church wanted me to start the job in September, right when my son was due. After discussing my health with my doctors, I'd decided that after he was born I would undergo a partial hysterectomy. The operation would hinder the HPV from growing into cancer, and I could breathe easier knowing it was at bay. I would not be able to have any more children, but I was okay with that. I discussed my delivery and surgery with the church staff, remaining vague about why I was having a hysterectomy. To my relief, they promised they would work with my schedule and let me start the position after I'd recovered.

In September, we welcomed our little boy, Carter, into the world. Pink and perfect, he was another reminder of God's amazing grace. Though I'd done nothing to deserve such goodness, God had lavished it on me anyhow. My children served as a reminder that God had truly forgiven me for my past. I did not need to keep looking back, because God didn't do that. He was only concerned with my heart right now, and I had completely given my heart to him.

I underwent the partial hysterectomy, and after recovering, I started my new job. As it turned out, my husband was right. I enjoyed every element of the job, from overseeing the church Web site to helping newcomers assimilate. My husband, a church insurance underwriter, provided a steady income as well. We fell into a happy rhythm with our two children, watching them grow from tiny newborns to active toddlers. Every day, I thanked God for giving me the opportunity to be a mother. At one dark point in my life, I'd wondered if I'd ever get married, much less have children. But God's blessings were abundant, and I did not take a single one of them for granted.

As time went by, I slowly opened up to a few of my peers at church, sharing my story with them. They were all very gracious and loving, and not one person wagged a judgmental finger in my face. I realized that I'd kept myself locked in a private hell for years, watching the world pass me by as I faced my shame alone. But the more I reached out, the more I discovered that everyone had something hard in his or her life. Many people who looked glossy and put together on the outside had, in fact, come from a troubled or painful past. Church was not a place full of perfect people — it was a place full of forgiven people.

The more comfortable I became with telling my story, the more I realized it needed to be told. Like many young girls, I had believed a lie. I had believed I would not be loved or feel normal unless I gave into premarital sex. I'd seen plenty of television shows, movies, magazines and billboards offering the idea that sex was casual, cheap and fun. I'd told myself sleeping around was really no big deal.

But in the process, I'd given away much more than my

body — I'd given away my heart. I knew many young girls struggled with the idea of giving up their virginity, yet they had no one to discuss their feelings with. Because sex was not discussed much at church, or even in their homes, they felt completely alone. *What if I could let them know they aren't alone at all?* I wondered. *What if they could see how valuable they are in God's eyes? What if they could believe that he cherishes them just as they are, that they don't need to sleep with some guy to feel important or loved?* If only they could glance down the road and see the emotional and physical damage a few nights of casual sex could instigate. If only I could help spare them the pain I'd endured and encourage them not to sell themselves short.

Though I'd spent much of my early life in the church, I'd never fully understood why God discussed sex in the Bible. He declared it was meant for one man and woman after they married, but the world had tainted that view, and I had bought into the idea that waiting for marriage was old-fashioned. Now, as a married adult trying to follow God's ways, I knew that God's design was best. Because he loved his children so much, he wanted to spare them from pain. I'd contracted HPV, but I'd been one of the lucky ones. My diagnosis could have been much more serious. But because of his grace, I now had two healthy children, daily reminders that he'd given me a beautiful second chance.

LOST AND FOUND

"Help is here. Where do you want us?" My aunt set down her buckets and smiled up at me.

"Thanks so much for coming. It was so nice of you," I told her.

My husband and I had just purchased a new house, and my aunt and uncle had showed up to help us clean. My father would soon be arriving with the trailer. I was so grateful not just for my immediate family, but for my extended family as well. They had been such a gift to me since I was a little girl. Though our family had walked away from the church for a while, I had never forgotten those early days at County Line Church. And through my aunt's persistence, I'd found myself walking through those doors years later, grateful to be home where I belonged.

I loved my job at the church and considered it a privilege to go to work each day. I'd found community at church and around my small town. The coffee shop had become a favorite spot of mine, and I looked forward not just to my perfectly brewed iced latte, but to chatting with the regular patrons as well. When I'd stepped into that coffee shop one day several years before, I'd been a distraught young woman at the end of her rope. My future had seemed bleak and lonely. But God had intervened, reminding me that he was indeed real and working in my life. He had seen the bigger picture even when I hadn't. And now I was living a life I'd never dared to dream of before. I could now hold my head high, knowing I'd found true fulfillment in God. He was the author of second chances, writing a beautiful story for me.

SHEENA'S SONG
The Story of Dennis McBrier
Written by Arlene Showalter

I breathed deep, like a football player just before the snap, while the lights of Chicago twinkled below us. My wife, Doris, sat beside me on the private jet; my son, Matthew, and daughter, Sheena, sat behind us. Realization hung in the silent air — *it's really happening. Now.*

అఅఅ

"I'll get straight to the point," Dr. Rich said. "Sheena needs a heart/lung transplant."

"How soon?" Doris gasped.

"Yesterday."

Sheena sat, wide-eyed. "And if I don't?"

"You'll die."

"Why heart *and* lungs?" Sheena asked.

"Because your condition, pulmonary hypertension, causes extra stress on the heart. Right side, to be exact. Your lungs are giving out, and the heart is worn out."

"What is the risk?"

"You're 17." Dr. Rich handed her a pamphlet. "Old enough to know for yourself what's involved."

The moment he left the room, Sheena turned to Doris and me. "You don't look shocked." She frowned. "Why?"

"We've known for some time that your condition would progressively get worse," Doris said. "But we didn't expect this. Or at least we hoped it wouldn't come to this."

"Why didn't you tell me before?" she demanded.

"The doctor told us not to limit you," Doris answered.

"What doctor?"

"Dr. Horowitz. He wanted you to live as normal a life as possible," I explained. "Besides, would it have made a difference if you knew?"

We returned to our home outside Kendallville, Indiana, and waited.

❧❧❧

In 1976, I worked at the local middle school. Three weeks before Doris was due to deliver our second child, I came home during my preparation class period and found her in labor. Our neighbor offered to watch our toddler son while I rushed Doris to the hospital.

I waited in the hallway until the nurse emerged from behind the double doors.

"You have a daughter," she said, grinning.

Nine days later, our family doctor, Dr. Chandler, met us in the nursery.

"Denny. Doris," he greeted us. "Could you come with me, please?" He led us into a small room nearby. "We need to discuss your baby's health."

Our baby's health? There's something wrong with Sheena?

"Please, sit down." Dr. Chandler gestured to two padded armchairs and then sat across from us.

"Your daughter," he said, fiddling with the stethoscope around his neck, "has a heart murmur — a loud one. I want you to take her to a pediatric specialist in Fort Wayne."

Heart murmur? I shuffled my feet. *What's a heart murmur? Is it serious?*

Doris and I returned home. I heard her calling her mother on the phone. "Hi, Mom … yes, we went to the hospital to see Sheena … what? Oh, yes, she's doing better. She's eating. What?" A long pause. "Why didn't you tell me before? Okay, Mom. Goodbye."

"What is it, dear?" I asked when she returned.

"Mom told me Dad had a heart murmur when he was born." Doris sat down. "I never knew."

That night we drove to Elmwood Mennonite Church.

"We need prayer for our baby," I said. "The doctor told us today that she has a heart murmur, and we have to take her to a specialist."

The people gathered around us like a human wall full of divine strength and asked God to heal our Sheena.

"We don't have a thing to worry about," I told Doris on the drive to Fort Wayne. "This doctor is going to confirm that there's nothing wrong with our baby girl."

We sat in the waiting room, surrounded by anxious parents, crying babies and bouncing toddlers.

God is all-powerful. He's healed our baby girl.

"McBrier?" The nurse called our name, clipboard in

hand. "Follow me, please." She led us into an examining room. After a short wait, the door flipped open.

"Mr. McBrier. Mrs. McBrier." He extended his hand, first to Doris and then to me. "How are we all doing today?"

"Fine!" I grinned. *Now, the doctor and the whole world will know the healing power of our God.*

The doctor bent over Sheena's tiny body, planting his stethoscope first here, then there. He cocked his head to one side as he listened, staring up at the corner of the wall where it meets the ceiling, and nodded.

"Yep," he said, straightening up. "It's a heart murmur, all right."

A heart murmur, all RIGHT? As in proof-positive-unhealed-present-tense heart murmur?

"We'll run an electrocardiogram just to make sure," he added.

We stumbled out into the late fall sunshine. Like a robot switched to autopilot, I maneuvered the car to the interstate and home.

"I don't know what to think," Doris said, looking at our tiny, precious, helpless bundle sleeping in her car seat. "I had such a peace that God had healed her."

My hands gripped the wheel. "So did I."

"Did we do something wrong?" Doris whispered.

"I ..." My brain whirled. "I don't think so."

Several miles melted away beneath the spinning tires.

"God is good." It was more a question than a statement.

"Yes," I agreed. "God is good."

"Then … then …" Doris swiped at a tear. "He must have a good reason for not healing our baby."

God's peace-filled presence flooded the car. "If he doesn't choose to heal Sheena," I said, "then he will get us through this."

༉ ༉ ༉

The doctor's office called to schedule Sheena's first heart catheterization when she was 18 months old. Again, we waited in a room filled with anxious parents and sick children.

"Mr. and Mrs. McBrier, I'm Dr. Horowitz."

"Please, Doctor," I said, "Denny and Doris."

He grinned. "Very well." The smile faded a bit. "We found a hole in the heart, in the septum between the left and right ventricles."

Doris and I stopped breathing.

A hole? In her heart?

"Not to worry," he said, widening his smile to reassure us. "It's known as Ventricular Septal Defect, or VSD." He chuckled. "Sounds ominous, I know, but really, it's a routine fix."

We relaxed — barely.

"Now," his tone turned brisk. "We can't operate until she's 40 to 45 pounds. Other than that, enjoy life. Just watch for signs of heart failure, and don't hesitate to call if you have any doubts or worries."

He stood up, and we shook hands. "Try not to worry."

God, if you brought us to this, I prayed, *you'll have to get us through it.*

I found myself pausing by Sheena's door in the night, straining to hear her even breathing.

❧ ❧ ❧

"Hey, honey," the nurse beckoned Sheena. "Jump up here on the scale. Hmmm …" She tapped the weights to the right. "Getting to be a big girl, you are." She grinned. "You're a whopping 38 pounds!"

Doris and I exchanged glances. *Almost 40 pounds.*

The summer before Sheena started kindergarten she reached the magic number.

"Dr. Horowitz is going to fix your heart, Sheena-Beena," I said the night before surgery.

" 'Cause it has a boo-boo?" she asked, her brown eyes round and shining.

"Yes, it has a boo-boo," I said. "A hole. Remember when you fell and tore a hole in the knee of your pants?"

Sheena nodded.

"What did Mommy do?"

"Mommy sewed it all up like new!" Sheena bounced her stuffed teddy bear on her lap.

"Right. So that's what Dr. Horowitz is going to do tomorrow," I said. "He's going to sew up that hole —"

"And make me all new!" She hugged the bear to her.

"Do you think Dr. Horowitz will see Jesus in there

when he opens up Sheena-Beena's heart?" I asked, tapping her tiny chest.

Sheena giggled.

৵৵৵

Dr. Horowitz scheduled heart catheterizations every three years after the open-heart surgery, to monitor the pulmonary pressure in her lungs. Every time, it increased. When Sheena was 13, he asked her to join us in the consultation room after her tests.

"Sheena," he said, "you're old enough to understand a little about your condition. It's called pulmonary hypertension." He leaned across the table to touch her hand. "You need to realize you can never bear children. Your heart couldn't take the stress."

Sheena sat, silent, chewing her lip. Then her chin rose. "Remember, Dad, how you told me that when you got cut from the Washington Redskins, you had a Plan B — your teaching degree?" She took a deep breath. "Well, now, I have a Plan B, too. I'll adopt."

৵৵৵

Sheena began her junior year as a normal teen, cheerleading, studying and hanging out with her friends. Normal until the day she fainted in Physical Education class.

Doris picked her up from school and scheduled a doctor's appointment. He sent us to Chicago.

LOST AND FOUND

That night, sitting alone in a motel room, Dr. Rich's words echoed in my head like a foghorn on Lake Michigan. *She'll die. She'll die. She'll die.* "Oh, God," I cried, pounding my knees with my fists. "I could lose my little girl! And there's not a single thing I can do about it."

I started pacing the cramped room. "I feel so helpless. So utterly and completely helpless."

"Do you trust me?" God asked in the stifled silence. "Do you know how much *I* love Sheena?"

"Yes, Lord," I said, sinking down on the bed. "I know you love Sheena, more than I do, and I know your ways are perfect. Not always understandable, but perfect. I put my daughter's life and future in your hands."

God's peace flooded the room. I slept.

৵৵৵

Dr. Rich put Sheena on a waiting list for double lung/heart transplants, and we returned home and tried to live as normal as possible in the months that followed. The phone rang, on Labor Day weekend, September 5, 1994, as Sheena ironed her school clothes.

"Hello … yes, this is Sheena … I'm feeling okay, I guess. What? Let me get my mom."

She handed off the phone and plopped down next to me, watching the 25th anniversary season opener of *Monday Night Football* with the San Francisco 49ers playing the Los Angeles Raiders.

"Dr. Garity says they have a possible donor." She

turned to me, tears flooding her eyes. "I hope the donor had time to find Jesus before he or she died."

Dr. Garity, a colleague of Dr. Rich, instructed Doris to get Sheena to the hospital ASAP. We drove to the Kendallville airport, where a private jet waited. A limousine met us on the tarmac in Chicago and raced us to Loyola University Hospital in Maywood, Illinois.

People gathered to support us during the long surgery: our pastor, Al, and his wife, Annie, Sheena's Aunt Janet and Uncle Mike, her two brothers, Brandon and Matthew. We prayed. We talked. But mostly, we waited.

"Everything looks good," Dr. Garity assured us, many hours later, with a weary grin. "Her vitals are good. You'll be able to see her when she comes out of recovery."

Our hopes soared for two days.

"Her white blood cell count is elevated," Dr. Garity said.

"What does that mean?" I asked.

"Acute rejection of the organs," he said.

"What can be done?" Doris asked.

"We'll give her steroids and cancer-fighting drugs," he said. "In transplants, we trade a condition that can't be controlled, that is defunct organs, with a condition that hopefully can be controlled with drugs. The purpose of these drugs is to suppress her immune system and avert rejection."

The hospital released Sheena 10 days later. We continued to battle the transplant rejection at home.

"You know, Sheena," I said one evening. "Your

mother rejected me at first, but she finally came around."

"Really?" she said. "How?"

"I moved to her town and started high school there as a freshman. Your mom thought I was a geek."

"No!" She giggled. "Why?"

"She didn't like my buzz-cut hair and thick glasses. And my pants were too short because I kept growing out of them." I grinned. "She told her best friend she could have me."

"How did you get Mom to change her mind?"

"Well, I thought your mom was cute, and I liked her calm demeanor, so I grew my hair out, got contacts and bought pants that fit. Didn't hurt that I was good at football, either."

"So, maybe my new heart and lungs will come around, too?"

"I got her to marry me, didn't I?"

❦❦❦

The organs refused to learn from my example. Sheena's face swelled from the steroids.

"I'm so ugly," she cried, looking in the mirror. "Look how fat my face is."

"It's temporary," Doris soothed. "When you're all better, it'll go away. The important thing is that you're still with us."

"I know," Sheena said. "I don't mean to be petty. I'm glad I'm here, too. We'll get through this together, right?"

I spent time with Sheena every evening. We talked about life, dreams and memories.

"Remember when you were 9," I started, "and I took you to see Grandma on my moped?"

"Of course!" Sheena's eyes shone. "We stopped for gas, and you bought me a candy bar."

"That was eight years ago! You remember what kind?" I teased.

"Bit-o-Honey." Her chin lifted. "Red and yellow wrapper. So there!" she said.

"I'm so ugly, now." Sheena's tone changed faster than a wide receiver running to the end zone.

"No, honey," I said. "Never ugly." I smiled. "What a tiny, beautiful baby you were."

"Tell me."

"I came home early to check on your mother because she'd gone into labor that morning."

"You like teaching middle school kids?" she interrupted.

"Most of the time." I laughed.

"Anyway, you weren't due for three weeks, but I found your mom in labor, so we dashed to the hospital. I think I hollered, 'Hold on, dear,' the whole ride over."

"Did I look … sick … when I was born?"

"No, honey," I said. "You were a beautiful, tiny baby doll."

"How tiny?"

"Five-pounds-2-ounces tiny."

"Did you see me born?"

"No," I said. "The nurse came out and told me, 'You have a beautiful girl.'"

"Were you allowed to hold me?"

"Yes. I couldn't stop stroking your itty-bitty fingers and toes." I halted. "We had no idea you had heart problems."

"How did you find out?"

"Well, you dropped to 4 pounds, 13 ounces, and the doctor wouldn't release you until you regained the weight you'd lost. Your mom and I came to the hospital every day to hold and feed you."

"Then what?"

"When you were 9 days old, the doctor took us aside and told us you had a heart murmur. Apparently, he ran tests to confirm suspicions he'd had before he told us."

"You had no idea?"

"Absolutely none."

Sheena fell quiet.

"You look tired, baby," I said, planting a kiss on her forehead. "Let's finish the story another time."

"Okay." She rested her head against the pillow and closed her eyes.

"So, what happened after you learned I had a heart murmur?" Sheena asked the following night. "Were you angry? Scared?"

"Scared," I said. "At that time, we went to the Elmwood Mennonite Church. Our pastor, Tony, and his wife, Ada, called other members of the church to support us. We prayed and prayed."

"For what?" Sheena asked.

"Do you know why we named you Sheena?" I asked, changing directions like a quarterback about to be sacked.

"Because it means *God is gracious.*" Sheena smiled.

"Exactly. Because God is gracious, we prayed that he would heal you of the heart murmur before going to the pediatric surgeon." I paused, rubbing my chin. "I — we fully expected Dr. Horowitz to announce he couldn't find any murmur."

Sheena squeezed my hand. "God knows what he's doing, doesn't he?"

"Yes." I swallowed. "Wasn't easy to accept it at the time, though. Your mother and I struggled through some serious shock first."

"But you got through it."

"Yes," I agreed. "I don't pretend to understand everything God allows, such as not healing you, and now, working on the transplant rejection, but I know he is always good."

ॐॐॐ

Two months passed. I sat down for our nightly chat.

"It seems like a hundred years since we went to Dr. Rich's office," Sheena said, "and heard him say, 'You need a lung transplant or you're going to die.'" She paused. "Not what a 17 year old expects to hear."

I reached for her hand. *What's this?* I thought, seeing my wife's engagement ring sparkling on her frail finger.

Sheena followed my eyes. "I hope you don't mind, Dad," she said, choking back a small sob. "I asked Mom if I could wear it. I know now I'll never have one of my own."

I blinked — hard.

Engagement rings come with a fiancé. A promise of marriage. Husband. Children. Sheena's grand goal in life. Family. Not to be.

Sheena squeezed my hand. "It's okay, Dad." She returned to her prior thoughts.

"I mean, here I was, just a normal person living a normal life and *BAM!* I'm facing transplant or death."

I nodded.

"I did a lot of thinking while waiting," Sheena said. "And praying."

Tears sprang up in my eyes.

"I thought about you and Mom, my brothers and my friends. I decided I was glad I was the one with the problem and not any of you."

I swallowed the standard-issue-football-sized lump in my throat, marveling at my beautiful daughter's even more beautiful spirit.

"God has given me all the strength I need to get through this," she said, patting my hand.

༺ ༺ ༺

"Listen to this," I said, popping a cassette into her machine. "Michele Peyton wrote this for you. She calls it

SHEENA'S SONG

'Sheena's Song.' She played it in church today, and I have a recording of it."

Sheena lay back and closed her dark eyes. Her dark hair fanned across the pillow's stark whiteness.

The Lord is my shepherd, He leadeth me
I have no wants, He fulfills all my needs
When I walk in the valley, He calls to me
Little Lamb, Little Lamb, Follow me

"I feel like God is a bazillion miles away, and he doesn't hear me," Sheena told me in early January, four months after the double transplant. "I don't even know what to pray for anymore."

I sat next to her and pressed her hand, feeling the hard gold of promised love still encircling her finger.

"I'm still in stinking rejection," she continued, staring up at the ceiling. "I thought God would have mercy on me."

I said nothing, for there was nothing to say. We filled the long night hours with silence and inane TV shows.

"Thank you, Daddy," Sheena said the next morning. "I'm sorry I kept you up all night."

"I'm okay," I said.

"But now you have to go to work."

"I'll manage."

"Thanks for being such a great dad." She sighed and nestled down into her covers.

"Lord," I prayed as I drove to the school. "You are our only hope. I know you have the power to heal Sheena, even yet, but as always, like Jesus, I can only pray, 'Your will be done.'"

I turned into the parking lot. "I only ask that you sustain us all through this and bring glory to the name of your son, Jesus." I choked back a sob. "Lord, I believe. Help me to believe."

৵৵৵

We watched our daughter's body's ceaseless fight against the life-sustaining organs. Its victory spelled her death. Sheena returned to the hospital in January.

The doctors called us in for a private conference. "You have a serious decision to make. Your daughter is in chronic rejection. Her only hope is a second transplant."

Doris and I looked at each other. "This is Sheena's call," I said, turning to Sheena.

"No," she said. "Can we go home now? I want to die at home."

"Look, Daddy," Sheena said. Her spirit remained strong even as her body weakened. "I read this today: 'For God has reserved a priceless inheritance for his children. It is kept in heaven for you, pure and undefiled, beyond the reach of change and decay. And God, in his mighty power, will protect you until you receive this salvation, because you are trusting him. It will be revealed on the last day for all to see'" (1 Peter 1:4, 5 NLT).

I tried to smile. I failed.

"Do you remember when I accepted Jesus into my heart?" she asked. "I thought everyone around me looked prettier and happier. I feel that way now." She pressed the Bible between her hands.

"I'm going to be with Jesus very soon," she continued, "but I can't help wondering what you and Mom and my brothers will do when I'm gone. I don't want you to be sad."

I choked back tears.

"I'm glad we didn't go for another transplant," she said. "It was the right decision."

⤳⤳⤳

I returned home from church Sunday, February 12, 1995, five months after the surgery, and went into Sheena's room.

"Are you sad, Daddy?" she asked.

I sat next to her bed. "I'm worried about you," I confessed.

"Don't you know what the Bible says about worry?" She reached for her Bible and began flipping pages. "Listen. 'Do not be anxious about anything, but in everything, by prayer and petition, with thanksgiving, present your requests to God. And the peace of God, which transcends all understanding, will guard your hearts and your minds in Christ Jesus'" (Philippians 4:6, 7). She looked at me.

"This morning I felt so defeated, but I prayed God

would touch my body according to his will." She smiled. "I'm ready for whatever happens."

Sheena lapsed into a coma the next morning.

I put her favorite song, "Agnus Dei" (Michael W. Smith), into the cassette recorder by her bed and pressed play: "Alleluia, Alleluia, For the Lord God Almighty reigns."

A single tear slid down Sheena's cheek and then God took her to be with him.

The high school allowed us to celebrate Sheena's life in the gymnasium. At the end of the service an invitation to know Jesus was given. No kids responded. Doris and I left the gym, but minutes later I returned. Around 80 classmates crowded around the youth pastors and counselors on the gym floor. Tears filled my eyes when I overheard some of their comments.

"I want to know Sheena's Jesus."

"I need God in my life."

"Life is uncertain. I want to know how to walk with God."

The enthusiasm of these young people poured healing salve over my broken, aching heart.

Then letters poured in. "Lest you think that Sheena's influence for the Lord has slowed, I want you to know it is only growing stronger … It's been wonderful to see the outpouring of God's Spirit on the lives of these kids."

"Sheena … was so crazy and so much fun to be around … She was so inspiring and had such a deep faith in God … It doesn't seem like she's gone, because spiritually she's not. But I can see her running and having the time of her new life with God. The thought of someday being able to talk to her and be with her is comforting and peaceful."

My hands shake a bit as I fold the letters and tuck them away in my Bible to read again.

I don't understand your ways, God, but I bow to them. Sheena's gone, but not her passion for Jesus. It lives on … in all these kids.

LOST AND FOUND

Sheena's Song
Written by Michele Payton

The Lord is my shepherd, He leadeth me
Into the pastures so peaceful and green
When I am thirsty He's always near
Providing the water so cool and clear

The Lord is my shepherd, He restores my soul
Leading me into the paths to be whole
He said He is with me wherever I go
Through valleys dark in death's shadows

The Lord is my shepherd, He prepares for me
A table in the presence of my enemies
My cup overflows with the oil He gives
And the promise of Love for as long as I live

The Lord wants to be your shepherd, too
Can you hear Him, He's gently calling you
As you walk in the valley He calls so sweet
Little Lamb, Little Lamb, Follow me.

The Lord is my shepherd, He leadeth me
I have no wants, He fulfills all my needs
When I walk in the valley He calls to me
Little Lamb, Little Lamb, Follow me

CONCLUSION

Do you ever wonder why we are capable of loving people so much? Some people believe love is a natural accident — a series of chemical reactions that cause us to feel. But I have to say, I'm not buying it. I believe God created us with the capacity to love.

For one thing, the Bible tells us that God IS love. If God is love and we were made in his image, why wouldn't he create us to love?

For another thing, God designed us with the capacity to love so we could love other people. In fact, at the very creation of the world, after God created Adam, he said, "It is not good for man to be alone" (Genesis 2:18a). So he created Eve to be Adam's partner. God created humans with the need to love and be loved.

But while God gave us the capacity to love, he also gave us the capacity not to love. If we're honest with ourselves, we could all probably name a few people we don't love or at least have a hard time loving. So why would God give us the capacity not to love? Think about it. If we have the capacity not to love, that means we have to make a choice to actually love someone. God didn't create us to be robots that just automatically love someone. With this capacity to choose to love or not love, God created the ability for us to have authentic relationships. So when you love someone and he or she loves you back, you can have confidence in that relationship. It means something. It's not superficial. It feels good to know someone else loves you that much, doesn't it?

I think the ultimate reason God gave us the capacity to choose to love was because of the desire he has to have a relationship with every person he has ever created. Sadly, a problem occurred in the first relationships he had with Adam and Eve. They messed up. And once they messed up, they broke the perfect relationships they had with a holy, perfect God. And that really bothered God. He wanted to fix that problem. And because God is a just God, he couldn't let that sin problem exist without punishment.

That's where Jesus comes in. Not just anyone could bear the weight and pay the price for the wrongdoings of all mankind. Only someone who lived a perfect life and was without sin could cover the grime of human weaknesses. Luckily, God sent his son, Jesus, to come to earth and live a perfect life. Though Jesus suffered and died a brutal, undeserved death on the cross, he did it to take the punishment for every wrong thing you've ever done. Maybe you've heard a thousand times that Jesus died for you. It's true. He came to take all your blame away. He came to cover all the shame, guilt and brokenness you feel right in this very moment. And it doesn't end there.

Jesus Christ conquered death. Three days after he died on the cross and was buried, he got up. He took the burdens of all the world on his shoulders, and sin couldn't even keep him in his grave.

Maybe all this time you've assumed that the God of Christianity was wrathful, sending everyone to hell that doesn't correctly check off his lists of do's and don'ts. You've picked up this book just in time for me to tell you that while hell is real, God's deepest desire is that you would choose to love him. Not because hell is a scary thought, but because God is good and he loves you more than you can imagine. He even died for you to prove it.

Following Jesus Christ is not an EASY path, but it is worth everything. If you believe that Jesus came and died to take your punishment, that he defeated death and lived again, God is inviting you to spend eternity with him in heaven. All you have to do is ask him to be with you now and guide you for the rest of your life. Will you trust him and commit to follow him now?

Here's a prayer to help get you started:

God, I believe that you sent Jesus to die for all the things I've done wrong in my life. I am not perfect, and I know I will always make mistakes. Will you forgive me for my past and please come into my life now? Will you reveal yourself and guide me as I live from day to day? Thank you for promising to love me even when I feel most unlovable. Amen.

Maybe life hasn't been going the way you dreamed it would. Please know that God is always ready to give you another chance to finish strong. It's never too late to find what you've been looking for. To be restored. To find hope and purpose. Like the open doors on the cover of this book, we often choose doors (paths in life) that lead to a dead end. Jesus talked about this in Matthew 7:13 and 14 when he said, "Enter through the narrow gate. For wide is the gate and broad is the road that leads to destruction, and many enter through it. But small is the gate and narrow the road that leads to life, and only a few find it." The world's door is wide and enticing, but it leads to a real "nowhere land." And while God's door might be narrow, it leads to the greatest life you could ever imagine.

Just like the people in this book, God's not done writing your story. You have a choice to seek Jesus and ask him to help you make good decisions. Find a Bible, and start reading it. If you don't have one, we'd be happy to give you one! We at County Line Church of God would love to walk alongside you as you continue on life's journey. Just remember, none of us at County Line is perfect or will ever pretend to be. We're all just sinners saved by the grace of Christ. When you enter our church, you are entering the "no-judgment zone." I hope we see you this Sunday!

Stuart Kruse
Senior Pastor
County Line Church of God

We would love for you to join us at County Line Church of God!

Check out our Sunday morning service times at our
Web site: www.countylinechurch.org.
Our address is:
7716 North County Line Road E, Auburn, IN 46706.

Please call us at 260.627.2482 for directions,
or contact us at www.countylinechurch.org.

For more information on reaching your city with
stories from your church, please contact
Good Catch Publishing at
www.goodcatchpublishing.com

GOOD CATCH
PUBLISHING

Did one of these stories touch you?
Did one of these real people move you to tears?
Tell us (and them) about it on our reader blog at
www.goodcatchpublishing.blogspot.com.